Development Site Evaluation

Macmillan Building and Surveying Series

Series Editor: Ivor H. Seeley

Emeritus Professor, Nottingham Polytechnic

Advanced Building Measurement, second edition, Ivor H. Seeley

Advanced Valuation Diane Butler and David Richmond

An Introduction to Building Services Christopher A. Howard

Applied Valuation Diane Butler

Asset Valuation Michael Rayner

Building Economics, third edition Ivor H. Seeley

Building Maintenance, second edition Ivor H. Seeley

Building Procurement Alan Turner

Building Quantities Explained, fourth edition Ivor H. Seeley

Building Surveys, Reports and Dilapidations Ivor H. Seeley

Building Technology, third edition Ivor H. Seeley

Civil Engineering Contract Administration and Control Ivor H. Seeley

Civil Engineering Quantities, fourth edition Ivor H. Seeley

Civil Engineering Specification, second edition Ivor H. Seeley

Computers and Quantity Surveyors A. J. Smith

Contract Planning and Contract Procedures B. Cooke

Contract Planning Case Studies B. Cooke

Design–Build Explained, D. E. L. Janssens

Development Site Evaluation, N. P. Taylor

Environmental Science in Building, second edition R. McMullan

Housing Associations Helen Cope

Introduction to Valuation D. Richmond

Marketing and Property People, Owen Bevan

Principles of Property Investment and Pricing W. D. Fraser

Property Investment Techniques, David Isaac and Terry Steley

Quality Assurance in Building Alan Griffith

Quantity Surveying Practice Ivor H. Seeley

Structural Detailing P. Newton

Urban Land Economics and Public Policy, fourth edition P. N. Balchin, J. L. Kieve and G. H. Bull

Urban Renewal – Theory and Practice Chris Couch

1980 JCT Standard Form of Building Contract, second edition   R. F. Fellows

Series Standing Order

If you would like to receive future titles in this series as they are published, you can make use of our standing order facility. To place a standing order please contact your bookseller or, in case of difficulty, write to us at the address below with your name and address and the name of the series. Please state with which title you wish to begin your standing order. (If you live outside the United Kingdom we may not have the rights for your area, in which case we will forward your order to the publisher concerned.)

Customer Services Department, Macmillan Distribution Ltd
Houndmills, Basingstoke, Hampshire, RG21 2XS, England.

Development Site Evaluation

N. P. Taylor

MA FRTPI ARICS

MACMILLAN

© N P Taylor 1991

First published 1991

1 0 3 7 7 5 0 6

Published by
MACMILLAN EDUCATION LTD
Houndmills, Basingstoke, Hampshire RG21 2XS
and London
Companies and representatives
throughout the world

Typeset by
Ponting–Green Publishing Services, London

Printed in Hong Kong

British Library Cataloguing in Publication Data
Taylor, N.P.
    Development site evaluation.
    I. Title
    333.77
    ISBN 0–333–51372–X
    ISBN 0–333–51373–8 pbk

17/02/92

Contents

List of Plans

Plans 2, 3, 4, 7, 8, 11, 12, 13 and 14 are based on Ordnance Survey maps and are reproduced with the permission of the controller of Her Majesty's Stationery Office © Crown Copyright

Preface

Anyone can find a site; the real skill is to be able to acquire it and know what the market is for the site. So I was told some years ago when giving a talk at a conference on site finding. There is a lot of truth in the observation, so why the need for a whole book on the subject? Well, it is all very well being able to buy a site and know that it is in a prime spot for the type of development proposed on it; but suppose the access to the site belongs to someone else, or the site was refused planning permission for a similar project in the recent past? Acquisition of the site or building without a careful check of the many factors that affects its development potential could prove to be a very expensive mistake. Of course, very few people do this because they know full well that various things need to be checked before they go ahead and buy. What this book attempts to do is to explain some of the factors that matter when one is evaluating a development site (which, incidentally, may include buildings as well as land).

Put in this way, the book would appear to benefit only prospective buyers of buildings or land. However, I hope it will also be of interest to planning officers, particularly those charged with the job of drawing up local plans in their area. All too often in the past plans have not paid sufficient regard to some of the site factors described in this book. The result has been that sites allocated for development in a local plan have remained dormant for many years or have been developed in a quite different way from that intended in the plan.

If this book helps to prevent such things happening it will have more than served its purpose.

I have benefited from the advice and help of many in the preparation of the book; in particular, Ian Trehearne, Peter Barefoot, David Foulkes and Graham Eves. My special thanks to them — the mistakes and omissions that remain are entirely my own.

This book is dedicated to my family who have had to put up with a lot during its preparation.

1 Introduction

The purpose of this book is to explain some of the factors that concern those who evaluate development sites. So who are these people, and why should they be interested in the evaluation of development sites? The people are local planning authorities, developers, financiers, property owners, plus their various advisers.

The reason for looking at these factors is simple. Property development is an important activity, it involves large sums of money, significant changes in property values and the end result, in the form of buildings, is of considerable interest to the public at large. Therefore it is important to 'get it right' at the outset, that is to say, when a site is being evaluated for its development potential. There is not much point in a developer investing heavily in the acquisition of a site if upon considered evaluation he discovers that it has no development prospects. Likewise the local authority in undertaking a local plan will wish to evaluate various sites in the plan area, in the light of planning criteria before they decide whether to propose them for development. This book is not concerned with the detailed appraisal of development submissions but it does point up the main factors that should inform the planning authority of whether the principle of development is acceptable.

This book is aimed principally at those who are directly involved in the development process and that includes the people listed above, – local authorities, developers, etc. It may also be of interest to the growing number of people who are concerned about development even though they themselves may not be involved in the process.

The factors considered in this book can for convenience's sake be divided into planning, marketing, legal, financial and physical factors. All of these have a bearing on the evaluation of development sites although some (such as marketing and financial factors) will concern the developer more than the local authority. Planning factors should concern all who are involved in the process for the simple reason that most development requires planning permission.

What is a Development Site?

This question needs to be asked because the term 'development site' includes many sites that people would not have regarded as such; they are not just the green fields on the edges of towns and villages. They are literally any land or property on which development will be undertaken and nowadays this often entails redevelopment, that is, buildings on land that already has, or had, buildings on it.

It will become apparent throughout this book that for a development to occur several hurdles have to be overcome, such as assembling the site into one ownership. First, it may not be large enough, without the addition of adjoining land in another party's ownership, to enable the desired development to take place. Second, the developer has to get planning permission which can be time consuming, expensive and uncertain. Third, he must assess the viability of the project before committing himself to substantial outlays. A development site will also have a different meaning according to whether it is being considered by the local planning authority or a prospective developer. This arises from the essentially different standpoints of the two parties. The local planning authority perceives a development site according to whether from a planning point of view the site should be developed or not. The developer's perspective is somewhat wider; he not only has to get planning permission; he must also be satisfied that he controls all the land necessary to carry out the development, that the development is profitable and finally that there is a market for it. Otherwise he will not develop it and to all intents and purposes he would not regard it as a development site.

It might be thought that the planning authority and developer could at least come to a similar conclusion on whether a site is a development site so far as the town planning aspect is concerned. This is not the case. Although there is a broad measure of agreement that certain areas, mostly Green Belts, cannot seriously be regarded as areas where development can occur, there is lively disagreement on many other areas or sites as to whether they constitute development sites from a planning point of view. This is because planning is not a scientific or objective process.

In the chapters that follow we shall look at a number of aspects which are essential to the evaluation of development sites: first, town planning. The policy framework of town plans is examined in Chapter 2, while the following chapter looks in more detail at a variety of town planning constraints. The significance of the town planning framework and planning constraints is that they largely determine whether permission is given by the local authority for the development that is contemplated on a site.

As well as establishing whether planning permission will be granted the developer will wish to know something of the physical characteristics of the site. Is the ground stable to build on? Is access possible? And so on. These questions are considered in Chapter 4. Ownership and legal constraints are also important and Chapter 5 deals with them. It looks at how to establish the ownership of a property and the nature of some of the legal constraints on property such as restrictive covenants and S106 Agreements. (The latter are agreements between the owner of a property and the local planning authority which impose an obligation on the owner to carry out certain works in conjunction with a development.)

Chapter 6 looks at the marketing of development. It describes various locational and land use characteristics of sites which have a bearing on one's assessment of the suitability of a site in marketing terms. For example, new hotels often need to be conveniently located near motorway or main road junctions so as to be easily accessible to guests.

Finally, Chapter 7 considers the economic viability of development proposals and puts forward a simple exposition of the residual valuation of a development project. This enables the developer to decide how much to offer for a site or property and it is therefore an essential part of the evaluation process. Chapter 7 concludes the 'technical' chapters of the book, while the final two chapters show how the technical processes are drawn together and what conclusions can be drawn about the whole process of development site evaluation.

2 The Policy Framework

This chapter deals with the planning policy aspects of site evaluation. They represent one of the most important factors when evaluating a site; if they mean that permission for development will be refused, they effectively rule out the site's being regarded as a development site.

The most certain way of determining whether a site has development potential from a planning point of view is to submit an application for planning permission to the local authority. Normally, a developer proposing to purchase a site will only purchase 'subject to planning', in other words, when planning permission has been given for the desired development. This is fine when the developer is certain of securing the site. However, on many occasions the developer is not so well placed. A site may be on the market with several purchasers vying for it; or the site is not on the market and the developer has a 'gut' feeling that it may have possibilities but wants an informed view. In such circumstances it may be imprudent to submit a planning application (which becomes a public document). What is needed is a reliable opinion on whether planning permission will be given. Armed with this opinion the developer may well feel confident to pursue negotiations with the site owner until he has secured an interest in the site. Then he can confidently go ahead and apply for permission.

Most of this and the next chapter will be concerned with how one arrives at a reliable opinion, but first it may be useful to explain who is the local authority to whom one applies for permission. Throughout England and Wales the application is normally made to the district or borough council in an area, rather than to the county council, although the latter may become involved in determining the application, for example, because of highway or strategic planning issues. It is worth mentioning two exceptions to this general rule, namely Joint Planning Boards and Urban Development Corporations. In the area of the Peak District and Lake District National Parks, the local planning authority is a Joint Planning Board which includes staff drawn from both the

5

relevant District and County Council and the Board. In other national parks the planning authority comprises a single committee with the national park officer and supporting staff.

Urban Development Corporations were first set up in 1981 in London Docklands and Merseyside and by 1989 11 had been established in England and Wales. They are listed below together with the area covered by each corporation.

UDC	Area (ha)
London Docklands	2 070
Merseyside	960
Trafford Park	1 267
Teesside	4 565
Tyne and Wear	2 375
Black Country	2 598
Central Manchester	187
Leeds	540
Sheffield	900
Bristol	360
Cardiff Bay	180

Their location is on Plan 1. Cardiff Bay is an exception in so far as Cardiff City Council, not the Development Corporation, is the authority to whom a planning application is made.

In areas of Urban Development Corporations the planning application is made to the Urban Development Corporation rather than to the district council. The task of getting planning permission may be eased in certain areas of the country known as Enterprise Zones and Simplified Planning Zones.

The former are designated by the Secretary of State and their locations are shown on Plan 1. Their purpose is to stimulate development within these zones; there are not only financial incentives to development (as described later), but also the procedure for obtaining planning permission is simplified. The application is made to the district council.

Likewise, Simplified Planning Zones (which are designated by local authorities) are areas where planning procedures for specified types of development have been simplified in the interests of promoting development. The application is made to the district council. Areas that are likely to be suitable for Simplified Planning Zone designation would in the words of Planning Policy Guidance Note 7 be:

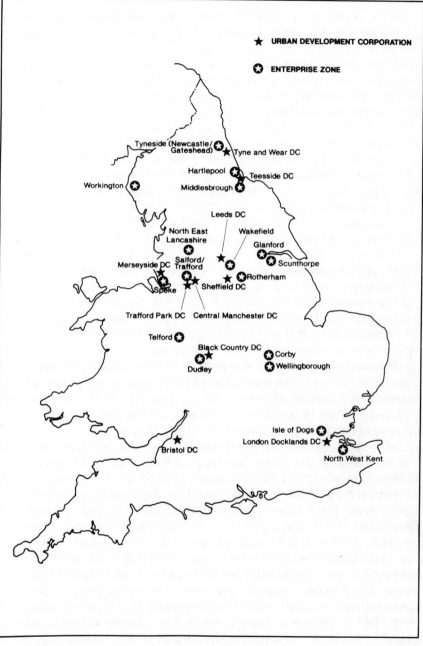

★ URBAN DEVELOPMENT CORPORATION

✪ ENTERPRISE ZONE

Tyneside (Newcastle/Gateshead) ✪★ Tyne and Wear DC

Hartlepool ✪★ Teesside DC

Workington ✪

Middlesbrough ✪

Leeds DC

North East Lancashire ✪

Wakefield

Glanford ✪ Scunthorpe

Merseyside DC

Salford/Trafford

Rotherham

Speke

Sheffield DC

Trafford Park DC   Central Manchester DC

Telford ✪

Black Country DC

Dudley ✪

Corby ✪

Wellingborough ✪

Isle of Dogs ✪

London Docklands DC ★

North West Kent ✪

Bristol DC ★

Plan 1 EZs/UDCs

older urban areas where there is a particular need to promote regeneration and to encourage economic activity.

For example, a major factory occupying 50–100 acres may have closed down, leaving the area derelict and forlorn. It is this sort of area whose regeneration the Government is anxious to promote. A good example is in Derby where two Simplified Planning Zones have been designated, one covering the area of the old Rolls-Royce works and the other the area of the Courtaulds Acetate Complex.

There are examples of Simplified Planning Zones in Derby, Corby, Birmingham Heartlands and Birmingham Kings Norton. In these areas it may not be necessary to seek planning permission for certain types of development, such as general industry (B2) business use (B1) and warehousing (B8). The planning regime for the particular zone will be specified by the local authority at the time of its designation.

With the exception of development in Simplified Planning Zones, applying for planning permission can be a hazardous and time-consuming business. However, it is possible to form a good idea of the likelihood of obtaining permission by undertaking a detailed evaluation of the planning constraints beforehand. This can save much time and trouble later on and also in certain cases it will have a direct effect on the way the planning application is worked up.

The evaluation needs to be undertaken in a methodical way and it is helpful to have a broad understanding of the ways in which planning constraints are expressed before we consider the constraints individually. They may be expressed in the form of planning guidance and this is published at national, county and district levels.

At a national level there is statutory and non-statutory guidance, the former comprising primary legislation, for example, the Town and Country Planning Act 1990, and secondary legislation, for example the Town and Country Planning (Listed Buildings and Buildings in Conservation Areas) Regulations 1987. The 1990 Planning Act is of little assistance in the evaluation of a site because it expresses general procedures relating to town planning and does not address matters of specific planning substance. Secondary legislation is also procedural, but may be far more specific, for example the listed buildings regulations, and this can assist the developer in deciding how he should proceed with an application. Of lesser authority, but arguably more important to the evaluation process, is non-statutory guidance, principally circulars, issued by the Department of the Environment, for example, Circular 15/84 — Land for Housing, Circular 14/84 — Green Belts.

Although of national coverage such circulars can be directly relevant to the evaluation of a specific site. The following examples illustrate the point. Circular 14/84 deals with Green Belts. The advice in the circular is that there is a strong presumption against development in Green Belts. If this advice is applied to a specific site in the Green Belt the consequences are plain.

Circular 16/87 deals with the use of farmland for development. It states that the need to retain farmland for its productive ability is less pressing now than it was after the Second World War. However, the need to keep the best and most versatile farmland free of development remains important. Therefore, a site of Grade 1 or 2 quality farmland will be unsuitable for development unless there are particularly compelling reasons to the contrary.

Also in this category one may include ministerial statements, for example a written answer in Parliament or a speech by a member of the Government on a particular planning aspect. Finally, there are two series of advice notes — Development Control Policy Notes and Planning Policy Guidance — which deal with particular aspects of planning, for example, development in the countryside, hotels, and so on.

Development Control Policy Note No. 12, for example, is entitled 'Hotels', and it sets out guidance on where new hotels should be sited. Paragraph 13 states that:

Some out of town sites may be particularly suitable for hotels and developers may be able to show that in the absence of any specific planning objections their proposals are warranted, for example, where an hotel would make use of an existing historic country house or where it could be sited in or adjacent to a group of existing buildings and would not create any significant additional impact on the landscape.

It is evident that the above advice can be directly applied to a specific site in order to evaluate the site's suitability for development.

The Note on hotels was published about 20 years ago but remains a valid piece of planning policy to this day. Other notes have been superseded by the more recent series entitled Planning Policy Guidance and eventually all DCPNs will be overtaken by PPGs.

Introduced in 1988, Planning Policy Guidance Notes bring together in convenient form various strands of existing Government advice on a particular topic. Thus they do not normally create policy but restate it in an easily accessible way. By 1990 some 15 statements had been published; these are listed below:

Planning Policy Guidance Notes

PPG1   General Policy and Principles (DOE/WO: January 1988)
        Outlines the planning framework and the purpose of the planning system. Contains a general statement of planning policy.
PPG2   Green Belts (DOE: January 1988)
        Explains the purpose of the Green Belts and the need for a general presumption against inappropriate development within Green Belts.
PPG3   Land for Housing (DOE: January 1988)
        Sets out the Government's policies on the provision of housing land and emphasises the key role of the planning system in meeting the demand for housing.
PPG4   Industrial and Commercial Development and Small Firms (DOE/WO: January 1988)
        Emphasises the importance of a positive and prompt approach towards applications which contribute to national and local economic activity.
PPG5   Simplified Planning Zones (DOE/WO: January 1988)
        Explains the working of this special procedure for facilitating development or redevelopment in designated areas by removing the need for a planning application for certain types of development proposals.
PPG6   Major Retail Development (DOE/WO: January 1988)
        Comments on recent retailing trends and provides policy guidance on planning and large new retail development.
PPG7   Rural Enterprise and Development (DOE/WO: January 1988)
        Contains advice on non-agricultural development in the countryside, including new uses of agricultural land and buildings, housing and the special restrictions which apply in some areas.
PPG8   Telecommunications (DOE/WO: January 1988)
        Gives comprehensive advice on planning aspects of telecommunications development.
PPG9** Regional Guidance for the South East (DOE: February 1989)

PPG10**   Strategic Guidance for the West Midlands (DOE: September 1988)

PPG11**   Strategic Guidance for Merseyside (DOE: October 1988)

PPG12   Local Plans (DOE/WO: November 1988)
Underlines the importance which the Government attaches to up-to-date local plans as the basis for sound and effective planning control and urges local authorities to extend the coverage of statutory local plans.

PPG13   Highways Considerations in Development Control (DOE/WO: November 1988)
Contains policy advice on the provision of accesses onto primary routes, parking, development conflicting with road proposals and provision of roadside services.

PPG14   Development on Unstable Land (DOE/WO: April 1990)
Seeks to clarify the position with respect to all forms of instability and their consideration within the planning system.

PPG15   Regional Planning Guidance, Structure and Plans and the Control of Development Plans.

** Will be reissued as Regional Planning Guidance in due course.

A parallel series of Planning Policy Guidance Notes deals with mineral policy guidance under the following headings:

Mineral Planning Guidance

MPG1   General Considerations and the Development Plan System (DOE/WO: January 1988)
Covers the general principles and policy considerations of minerals planning with specific advice on the development plan system.

MPG2   Applications, Permissions and Conditions (DOE/WO: January 1989)
Provides guidance on planning applications for minerals development, planning permissions and the imposition of planning conditions.

MPG3   Open-cast Coal Mining (DOE/WO: May 1988)
Provides advice to mineral planning authorities and indicates national policy considerations on the exercise of planning control over open-cast coal mining.

MPG4   The Review of Mineral Working Sites (DOE/WO: September 1988)

Provides guidance on the review of mineral working sites, including the compensation implications.

MPG5   Minerals Planning and the General Development Order (DOE/WO: December 1988)

Provides guidance on those aspects of the General Development Order which are of special relevance to minerals interests.

MPG6   Guidelines for Aggregates Provisions in England and Wales (DOE/WO: March 1989)

Provides advice on how to ensure that the construction industry continues to receive an adequate and steady supply of minerals at the optimum balance of social, environmental and economic costs.

MPG7   The Reclamation of Mineral Workings (DOE/WO: August 1989)

Gives advice on planning considerations, consultations and conditions which are relevant to the reclamation of mineral workings.

Regional Planning Guidance

RPG1   Strategic Guidance for Tyne and Wear (DOE: June 1989)
RPG2   Strategic Guidance for West Yorkshire (DOE: September 1989)
RPG3   Strategic Guidance for London (DOE: September 1989)
RPG4   Strategic Guidance for Manchester (DOE: December 1989)
RPG5   Strategic Guidance for South Yorkshire (DOE: December 1989)

To illustrate their relevance to the evaluation of a site one may take as an example PPG3: 'Land for Housing'. This states that: 'in many villages provision can be made for modest development without damage to the countryside ... Expansion of villages and towns into the surrounding countryside is ... objectionable if it creates ribbons or isolated products of development'.

The guidance in the Note is not specific to a site but it does help one to assess whether a site may be suitable for development (subject to any other planning policies that may apply in the area). Thus site A on Plan 2 might comply with the guidance, whereas site B almost certainly does not because its development would create a ribbon of housing into the countryside.

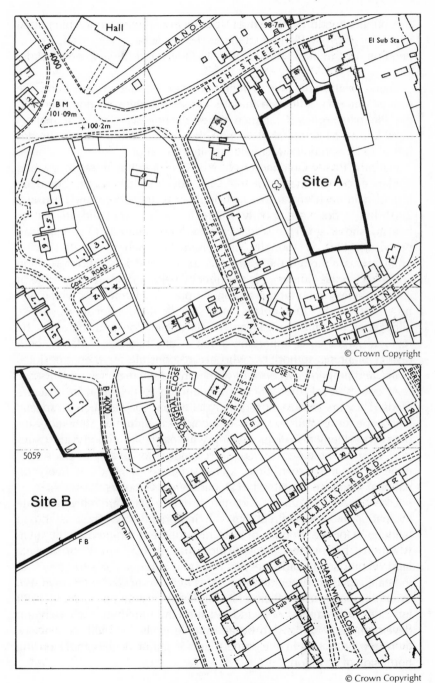

© Crown Copyright

© Crown Copyright

Plan 2 Village sites

A publication in 1990 by the Department of the Environment entitled 'Index of Current Planning Guidance' provides a very useful compendium of Circulars, PPGs, DCPNs, MPGs and RPGs (see Appendix 1).

There is little guidance at regional level that has a bearing on site evaluation; what guidance there is comes mainly from documents in the Planning Policy Guidance series dealing with regional matters (now known as Regional Planning Guidance) and they are too 'broad-brush' to be of much direct value in site evaluation.

Planning Policy Guidance Note No. 11, for example, sets out broad guidance for Merseyside. It indicates how much housing should be provided in each of the five metropolitan districts between 1986 and 2001 but it does not specify where in each district the amount of housing should go. The Guidance also draws attention to certain road proposals, not yet formally programmed, which have site-specific implications although these are not spelt out. While the information contained in the Guidance is not directly helpful in evaluating a site, it is nevertheless important in setting the planning framework which will be translated by local plans into specific land allocations. These allocations are directly relevant to site evaluation and therefore the regional guidance is important, albeit at one remove. Certainly, both district planning authorities, who are responsible for preparing local plans, and property owners will wish to heed the regional guidance.

At county level, the principal guidance is to be found in structure plans. They are important for their definition of areas such as special landscape or coastline, areas of ecological value or strategic gaps between settlements. Plans dealing with particular countryside issues may also be prepared by county councils, for example landscape, minerals or the Green Belt. Many structure plans draw freely on national guidance contained in Departmental Circulars.

Like Regional Planning Guidance, structure plans are relevant to site evaluation in a less direct but still important way. They set broad guidelines for the amount of new development required in the area, whether it be business, general industrial or retail space, or housing land. While such guidelines do not specify particular sites they can indicate whether a specific proposal is likely to accord with them. For example, the Structure Plan for North East Wiltshire approved in 1988 indicates an area west of Swindon called the rural buffer where major development is unlikely to be acceptable to the Council; conversely, there are proposals in the same plan for major development on the north side of Swindon.

Structure plans are also important in respect of road proposals. They specify major road proposals in their area and provide the basis for the county council's transport policies and programme. This is an annual report of the council listing in more detail the various road proposals, together with the likely timing of their construction. It is important to remember that the transport policies and programme is not a policy-making document but derives its basis from the structure plan for the area. The transport policies and programme includes details of roads under construction at the time of publication, together with a 5-year programme of new roads and preparation list of new roads. Finally, there is a reserve list which is set out in an order of priority but for which there is no specific timetable.

Neither the structure plan nor the transport policies and programme contains plans showing precisely where roads will go. Usually it is possible to examine such plans at the county council offices once the road line has been fixed.

The sequence of drawing up and fixing a road line is obviously important to landowners and developers because often the road line has a powerful effect on where future development may occur. In the case of the landowner he may well be keen to see one particular route adopted in order that part or all of his landholding becomes suitable for development. Likewise, the developer who is considering the potential of a site will closely examine the route options in an area to see how they affect his site, and he will find out exactly when the chosen route is published.

To give a 'real-world' example, there was considerable interest in the late 1980s in the proposed Hereford bypass. In 1987 the Department of Transport published a statement outlining two alternative routes for the bypass, one around the east of the town, the other around the west (see Plan 3).

If the eastern option was chosen (as it eventually was) areas such as Holmer would become ripe for development. If the western option was chosen they would not.

The Department's choice is, not surprisingly, kept strictly confidential until an official publication date. Therefore, a developer may well take expert advice from a highway engineer on where the route is likely to go and he may invest in acquisition of a site on the strength of this advice. The alternative is to wait for the Department to announce its preferred route and then compete with perhaps many other developers to acquire sites on the 'right' side of town.

At the local level there is a wide range of plans drawn up by district

The Alternative Routes

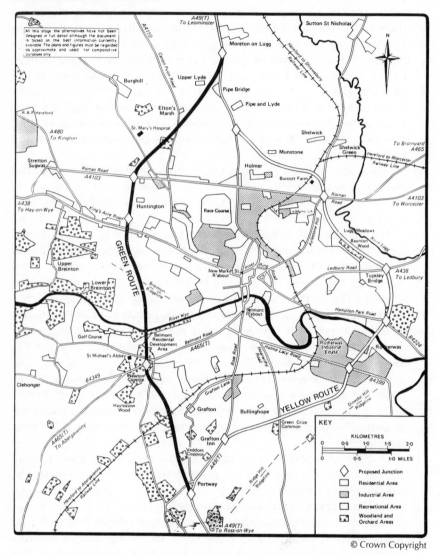

© Crown Copyright

Which alternative do you prefer?

Plan 3 Hereford bypass options

and borough councils. Some relate to a whole district, others to a part; some are statutory, others informal; some run to hundreds of pages while others could almost have been done on the back of a cigarette packet. Yet despite their multifarious nature local plans are often of the greatest importance when it comes to evaluating a site; this is because they are site-specific plans. One can consult a local plan and, as often as not, work out what particular policy or proposal affects the land that one is assessing.

In the County of Avon there were in 1990 no less than 18 local plans which had either been approved or were being prepared. They covered extensive rural areas or compact town centres. The City of Bath for example covers an area just 6 km by 6 km. A person living in the Kingsmead area of the city would see that the Local Plan designates the following policies for the area:

(1) Conservation Area (where extra control is imposed on the appearance of development proposals).
(2) Site on the south side of Monmouth Place is proposed for housing.
(3) The Percy Boy's Club is to be relocated when an alternative site can be found, and the club will be redeveloped for housing.
(4) The business at 208 Monmouth Place could expand eastwards along the road.

These policies are depicted on a map, on which Plan 4 is based and they give immediate, albeit not necessarily comprehensive guidance into the development possibilities of a site.

The structure and local plan system covers most, but not all, of the country. The exceptions are the old metropolitan counties which were disbanded in 1986. They include West Midlands, West Yorkshire, South Yorkshire, Merseyside, Tyne and Wear, Greater London, Greater Manchester. The successor authorities to the counties are required to prepare unitary development plans which combine some of the features of both structure and local plans.

They include site-specific proposals and policies and, as well as a detailed report, they contain a map on an Ordnance Survey base showing where the policies and proposals have effect. However, the plan is less comprehensive than a structure plan at the strategic level; and less detailed than a local plan at the local level. Thus, the proposals map of the Birmingham Unitary Development Plan is at a scale of 1:25000, whereas many local plans are at a larger scale. It is

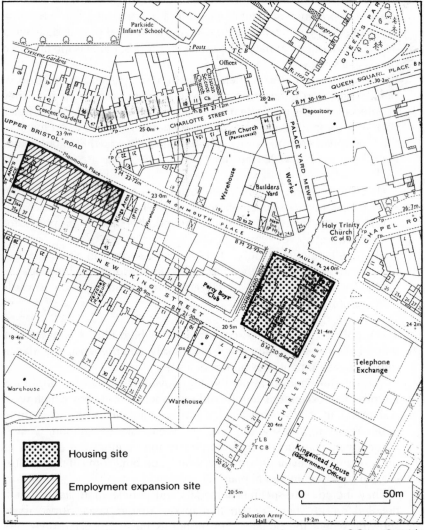

Plan 4 Bath city centre local plan

not possible to identify individual property boundaries in the Unitary Development Plan, and the proposals contained in it do not have the same precision as in a local plan.

In 1989 the Government announced proposals for changing the system of structure and local plans in England (see 'The Future of Development Plans' Cm569, HMSO). At county level county statements would replace structure plans; they would be more concise and more clearly restricted to matters that were genuinely of countywide importance.

At district level, district development plans would replace local plans and they would cover the entire area of a local authority, rather than as at present, when many plans cover only part of an area.

In September 1990 the Secretary of State for the Environment indicated that he would not be putting the White Paper proposals precisely into effect. He would attempt to speed up the system of plan preparation by reducing the role of the Department of the Environment in the process, but structure plans would remain. Many local authorities are preparing local plans which in fact cover their entire area and there is no doubt that they will be the principal source of advice for site evaluation.

The final level in the policy framework comprises 'Supplementary Planning Guidance' to use the term mentioned in the Local Plans Memorandum (see Department of the Environment Circular 22/84). This encompasses a variety of plans and policies usually in the form of development briefs for a specific site or a policy on a particular subject, for example conversion of farm buildings. Where a development brief has been drawn up for the site being assessed it will clearly be of particular relevance. It is likely to indicate the preferred uses for the site, the density of development, means of access, landscaping and any other planning restrictions — all aspects of vital concern to whether a developer wishes to acquire and develop the site.

One should also check the status of a plan. There is a world of difference between a statutory, adopted local plan that has been the subject of public consultation and debate and a non-statutory, informal plan drawn up without public involvement. The former carries much more weight in the assessment of a site's development potential. As Planning Policy Guidance Note No. 1, dealing with general principles of planning states:

Where the plan is up to date and relevant to the particular proposal, it follows that the plan should normally be given considerable weight in the decision (on whether a scheme is permissible by the planning authority) and strong contrary planning grounds will have to be demonstrated to justify a proposal which conflicts with it.

The informal plan on the other hand carries less weight and the developer may well feel that it is open to challenge. For example, an informal plan for part of Devizes town centre in Wiltshire indicated that redevelopment proposals for shopping purposes should be restricted to shops selling non-food items. In the event the developer put forward proposals for a large food store and these have been approved.

To sum up, in any evaluation of a site it is most important to consult the various plans for the area, making sure, incidentally, whether they are up to date, relevant or about to be superseded. The local authority offices will normally be the first port of call in undertaking this part of the evaluation and the planning officer, if you can get hold of him, will be a valuable source of information for the relevant plans.

The evaluation of development sites from a planning point of view is not simply a matter of consulting a structure or local plan and seeing whether the proposed development accords with the plan or not. First, there may not be an up-to-date local plan for the area; second, the plan is an important factor, but not the only one, when it comes to deciding whether planning permission will be obtained for the developer's proposals. Both of these matters will now be examined in more detail.

First of all, is there an up-to-date local plan for the area? The emphasis is on local rather than structure plans because the latter are of limited value when evaluating development potential. If there is an up-to-date local plan for the area, that will carry a lot of weight in any evaluation, but if there is not there may be scope to obtain permission for the desired scheme simply by submission of a planning application in what is a policy vacuum. On the other hand, if a new local plan is in the offing, it will be prudent to request the local authority to cater for the developer's requirements in the preparation of the plan. This approach takes time and there is no guarantee of success. However, if no action is taken the local plan may come up with policies or proposals which prevent the site being developed in the way that the developer desires.

Although it is important in one's evaluation of a development site, the local plan is not the only planning factor to be taken into account. What will be the effect of a proposed development on local public opinion? The latter can have a powerful effect on whether planning permission is forthcoming for a scheme. This requires most careful analysis as part of the evaluation process. Of particular importance in regard to schemes in residential areas are the effects on traffic and property values. Accordingly, one needs to examine the means of access to a site in case it involves drawing additional traffic along residential streets. With regard to property values, house owners are of course, particularly sensitive and they will strongly object to schemes if they think that they will devalue their properties. One therefore needs to consider whether a development proposal can be presented in a way that will not cause major local controversy and this is likely to involve a variety of public relations activities which are beyond the scope of this book. The lesson is that a favourable policy framework may not be sufficient to ensure a quick permission for a scheme and one should never underestimate the effect of an adverse publicity campaign.

Sometimes a site, whether greenfield or developed, has a planning 'history' and this can be very important to one's evaluation of the site's potential. The planning history of a site consists of previous applications for development on the site. The applications may have been approved or refused and if the latter they may then have been the subject of an appeal to the Secretary of State for the Environment. As well as applications for planning permission, the site may have been the subject of applications for Listed Building Consent, an Established Use Certificate or Certificate of Appropriate Alternative Development. The outcome of such applications is critical. If an application for a five-storey office building on the site was refused on the grounds of over intense development it will indicate that some development may well be acceptable, albeit not at five storeys. Alternatively, if an application for housing was refused, appealed and dismissed on appeal, because of loss of good quality farmland, that has obvious implications for any similar proposals on the site.

The site history needs to be examined with care and understanding, as the above examples testify. It may deter a developer completely or may point him in the direction of a different type of development from that previously submitted to the council. From the council's point of view they too should have regard to site history when drawing up a plan for their area. If they refused proposals for a site solely on the grounds of prematurity in advance of a local plan, it may well be appropriate now to consider such a site for development.

The validity of different chapters in the site history must be carefully checked. In particular it is necessary to establish whether there are any planning permissions that are still 'live'. These are permissions which, though not put into effect, were nevertheless granted within the previous three years, in the case of an outline permission, or five years in the case of a full permission.

If a permission has lapsed through the passage of time it ceases to be a valid part of the site history, but this is not to say that it loses all relevance to one's appraisal. This is because it is a well established principle of planning that if a particular form of development was considered acceptable at some time in the past then, unless there has been a material change in planning circumstances since that time, permission should again be forthcoming. Some structure and local plans have even formalised this view with specific policies.

3 Planning Constraints

A convenient way of considering planning aspects is to look at the various constraints which normally exercise the minds of town planners when they draw up their plans for an area or process planning applications. Although by no means exhaustive the following constraints could be looked on as a useful check list.

There are a variety of countryside restraints which planning authorities operate throughout the country. Although such constraints tend to affect greenfield development rather than redevelopment proposals, that is not always the case. The following text describes some of the better known constraints.

Green Belts

Green Belts covered approximately 1.8 million ha of land in England and Wales in 1988. In any evaluation of sites, they represent one of the most important factors to be taken into account. Despite constant pressure from development, especially in the South East, the amount of land affected by Green Belts has more than doubled in the period from 1979, when they covered 730 000 ha, to 1988. In Scotland on the other hand the amount of land covered by Green Belt has declined from 218 000 ha in 1979 to 203 000 ha in 1990, due largely to the abolition of the Dundee Green Belt in 1982.

Green Belts were first described in the Ministry of Housing and Local Government Circulars 42/55 and 50/57 and have been endorsed in Department of the Environment Circular 14/84 and Planning Policy Guidance Note No. 2. The purposes of them are well known and are set out in the Circular and in essence they have four main functions: namely, to prevent the outward spread of towns; to safeguard the surrounding countryside from further encroachment; to prevent towns from merging into one another; to preserve the special character of historic towns and to assist urban regeneration. This last function was added in 1984 as a result of Government concern about the inner cities.

The Green Belt round London is probably the best known and it varies in width from about 11 to 24 km (7–15 miles) even though parts of it are highly fragmented. The inner boundary of the Green Belt follows roughly the outer edge of the built-up area of London and the outer boundary is some 11 to 24 km (7–15 miles) further out. There are 'holes' within the Green Belt where there were already larger settlements at the time of designation and the edge of these settlements also forms an inner boundary to the Green Belt. Most Green Belt land is open countryside but it may include buildings and even small settlements within it. Especially round London there is open land of no scenic beauty which is included in the Green Belt. It may be a disused gravel pit, the site of illegal tipping or an area criss-crossed by power lines, roads and railways. Despite the unsatisfactory appearance of such areas the Government made it plain that they may still serve a Green Belt function, for example, to prevent coalescence of settlements within the Green Belt.

Once a Green Belt has been established the advice of the Government is that it should remain. Permanency is an essential feature of the Green Belt and this applies particularly to its edges which are the parts more likely to be under pressure for development than land wholly surrounded by Green Belt.

Apart from the metropolitan Green Belt round London there are Green Belts round many of the larger cities in Great Britain, for example, Glasgow, Oxford, Bristol and Manchester. Plan 5 shows the location of Green Belts in England based on approved structure plans in September 1987. In most cases the boundaries of the Green Belt are clearly defined on detailed maps which typically are at a scale of 1: 2 500 or 1:25 000. One can therefore ascertain without too much difficulty whether or not a site lies within the statutory Green Belt. In some areas though, for example Oxford, the precise boundary of the Green Belt has not been determined despite the fact that the general extent of the Green Belt is known. As local authorities normally operate an 'interim Green Belt' policy in such areas, this represents as effective a constraint on development as a fully detailed policy.

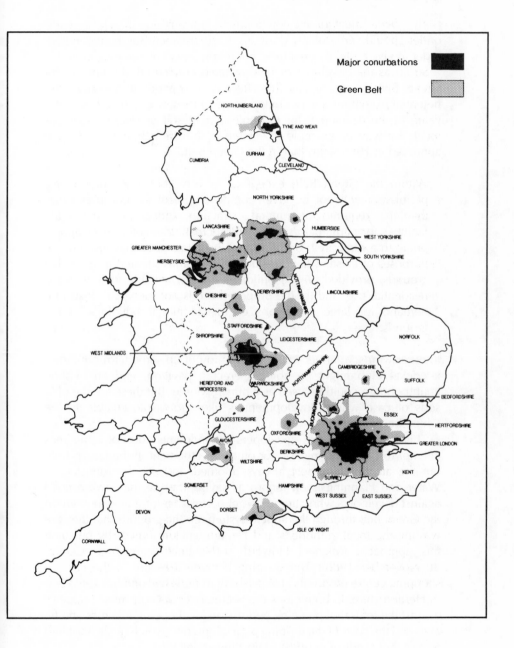

Plan 5 Green belts

The Department of the Environment are anxious that local authorities should very quickly draw up detailed Green Belt boundaries in order to give certainty on a most important aspect of planning policy.

So far as the developer or landowner is concerned, the notation of Green Belt on a site has the effect of ruling out its development potential except for a very limited range of uses, uses which have little value to the developer, for example agricultural or forestry development. By way of example, the Hertfordshire Structure Plan Review approved in 1988 states that in the Green Belt:

> Within the Green Belt, except ... in very special circumstances, permission will not be given for development for purposes other than that required for mineral extraction, agriculture, small scale facilities for participatory sport and recreation, or other uses appropriate to a rural area; or the use for hospitals or similar institutional purposes of existing large residential buildings situated in extensive grounds, provided (a) the buildings are not suitable for continued residential use, and (b) the proposed use is not such as to lead to a demand for large extensions or for additional buildings in the grounds.

In other words, a farmer might be able to put up some farm buildings, a cricket club might be able to erect a pavilion, and an existing country house could be used as a nursing home. But these are the only sorts of case where development is likely to be acceptable in the Green Belt.

This is not to say that developers or landowners do not sometimes attempt to obtain permission for other development in the Green Belt, but the attempt is almost always doomed. Indeed, the Minister for Water and Planning is on record as saying that he may award costs against developers who attempt to get permission for a development in the Green Belt through the appeal system, on the grounds that they are wasting the local authority's and Department's resources by pursuing this approach. (Michael Howard at National Agricultural Centre, 30 November 1988.) The warning became a reality in the case of shopping centre proposals at Wraysbury in Berkshire and Bricket Wood in Hertfordshire. In both cases the Secretary of State dismissed appeals against the refusal of planning permission for shopping schemes and he awarded the costs of the ensuing public inquiries (which ran at least into tens of thousands of pounds) against the appellants.

National Parks

There are now 11 national parks in England and Wales and they were set up under the National Parks and Access to the Countryside Act 1949. The most recent of the 11 parks was established on 1 April 1989 in the Norfolk Broads. Although much of the area covered by National Parks is unlikely to be of interest to developers of housing, commercial or industrial property, it is worth noting the geographic extent of the parks since they do abut some major towns or cities where pressures for this type of development may exist. Plan 6 shows their extent.

In national parks the overriding criterion is the preservation of their natural beauty. This does not mean that no development may occur, but it is likely to be for tourist or leisure purposes where it is permitted.

In this respect there is general guidance in a publication by the Countryside Commission which looks at the types of constraint which should apply to proposals for tourist development. (See Countryside Commission/English Tourist Board Principles for Tourism in National Parks, September 1989). Although couched in general terms the policy guidance has some value in helping to decide whether a site may be appropriate for development. The guidance points out that:

(1) the scale of development must be appropriate to the setting;
(2) the development should respect the capacity of the immediate site and surrounding landscape to absorb visitors;
(3) development which brings sympathetic new uses to historic buildings or derelict sites may be welcomed.

In evaluating a site for say a holiday park, or marina, the prospective developer will wish to pay careful attention to these principles or whatever more detailed principles and policies occur locally.

Areas of Outstanding Natural Beauty

These areas are more extensive than national parks and in 1985 they covered 1.7 million ha of England and Wales. At this time there were 35 such areas. They are designated by the Countryside Commission under Section 87 of the National Parks and Access to the Countryside Act 1949.

Like national parks they largely cover rural areas (see Plan 6) but

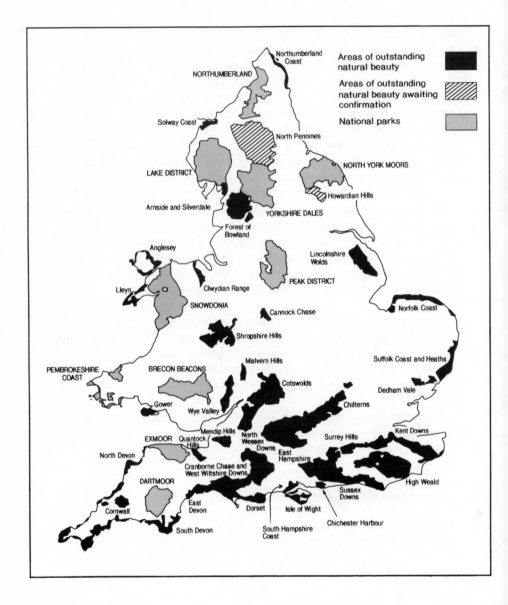

Plan 6 AONBs National parks

they also adjoin or even include towns. In Kent for example the area north and west of Folkestone is covered by the Kent Downs Area of Outstanding Natural Beauty.

The existence of the designation does not prevent development from occurring. Using the same example from Kent, the County Council have proposed development of some 1 400 houses and 10 ha of employment land at Hawkinge, all of which lies in the Area. In addition, proposals of national importance, such as the Channel Tunnel, may necessitate works in an Area of Outstanding Natural Beauty, whether it is the terminal facilities alongside the Channel Tunnel or a high-speed rail link connecting to London. Likewise, the town of Ross on Wye in Hereford and Worcester, is entirely contained within the Area of Outstanding Natural Beauty designation, but this has not prevented the allocation of substantial areas for new housing and employment uses.

The Countryside Commission have published a policy statement on development in such Areas and the key paragraph (22) reads as follows:

i)   (Not relevant);
ii)   New major industrial or commercial development should be regarded as inconsistent with the aims of designation, except where it is proven that such developments are in the national interest and no alternative sites are available;
iii)   Applications for substantial new mineral workings, or extensions to existing workings in AONBs should be subject to the most rigorous examination to assess the need for the minerals and the environmental effects of the proposal;
iv)   (Not relevant);
v)   Extension or creation of small scale industries or commercial units within, or immediately adjacent to, towns and villages in AONBs should, where permitted, be in sympathy with the architecture and landscape of the area.

CCP Areas of Outstanding Natural Beauty: A policy statement.

Areas of Landscape Value

County councils employ numerous titles for areas of landscape which they wish to protect. For example, in Hertfordshire there are

Landscape Conservation Areas, and Landscape Development Areas. In Essex there are Countryside Conservation Areas and Special Landscape Areas and in Cornwall there are Areas of Great Landscape Value, Special Areas of Great Landscape Value, and a Heritage Coast Area.

Such designations represent a further constraint on development although they may be used more as a device for bureaucratic control than representing an objective evaluation of the importance of landscape. What do they mean in practice, so far as development potential is concerned? The wording of the policies is not encouraging. The Countryside Conservation Area in Essex for example is an area where: there will be a presumption against additional development other than that essential to agriculture, forestry or recreation.

In Cornwall the plan states that in the designated areas: there will be a presumption against development which would adversely affect the amenity and landscape character of the area.

The wording of the policies is vague and leaves considerable discretion to the local authority planner. In reality, though, these countryside designations are rolled back where the demands of development, as interpreted through the structure plan for the area, required it. The role of the structure plan needs emphasising. It is not sufficient to assert that development of a site covered by one of the above landscape designations is acceptable because it has occurred elsewhere in the area. It is essential to demonstrate that there is a need for more housing or employment or shopping land in accordance with the requirements identified by the structure plan. In short, special landscape notations on a site do not preclude its development potential but they do mean that a development plan justification is necessary to underpin a development proposal.

Strategic Gaps

The concept of strategic gaps is crucial to evaluating greenfield development proposals in the more populous parts of the country. It is a concept which was being used more and more in the late 1980s and is likely to remain, if not increase, in the future. The underlying objective of strategic gaps is to prevent settlements from coalescing. It is not a block on development provided that such development does not cause coalescence. The Secretary of State made this clear when he approved the West Sussex Structure Plan (Alteration No. 1) in 1988.

It is often possible to identify whether a piece of land falls within a strategic gap by consulting the local plan for the area. For example the Loddon Valley Local Plan, covering a part of central Berkshire, shows on plan the extent of several gaps which were described in outline only in the Berkshire Structure Plan. An extract of the plan with the relevant notation appears in Plan 7.

In the event that a site falls within a strategic gap it will be necessary to consider whether the development which the developer is proposing causes coalescence. This might well be the case with a proposal occupying much of the site area, such as housing, but if the scheme was a free-standing building in a largely undeveloped setting, for

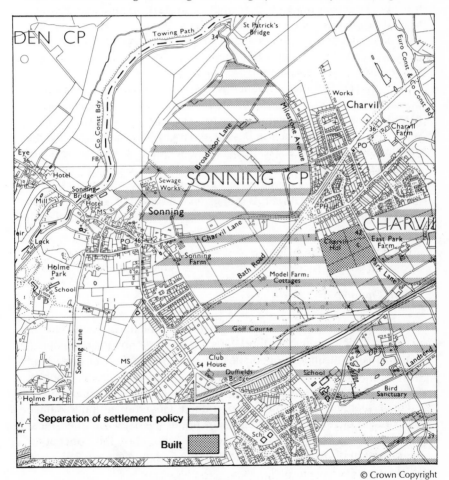

© Crown Copyright

Plan 7 Strategic gap

example, a headquarters building or hotel, it might well be argued that it would not cause coalescence. A good example of such thinking can be found in the decision by the Secretary of State on an appeal for an office and warehouse building on the edge of Swindon. The site of the building lay within a strategic gap between Swindon and the town of Wootton Bassett some 2 km to the south west. At its narrowest point the gap was only 1.9 km wide and it was at this point that the proposed building was to be sited. The proposal was rejected by the Local Authority. When the matter had been debated at a public inquiry, following an appeal by the applicant, the Inquiry Inspector stated that the gap policy imposed a presumption against development which tended to lead to the coalescence of Swindon and Wootton Bassett. It was not the same as a Green Belt policy. The applicants wished to construct an extremely large building with a footprint of 5.7 ha but they had offered a landscape buffer on one boundary. Both sides at the inquiry agreed that mere distance was not the only factor to take into account in the gap; the Inspector thought it was the perception of the gap that was the most significant factor. The question was whether the separate identities of Wootton Bassett and Swindon would remain if the development took place. The Inspector concluded, and the Secretary of State agreed, that the development would not harm the gap and therefore the appeal was allowed. Of course, every proposal in a gap has to be looked at on its merits but, given the spread of 'gap' policies in structure and local plans, it is as well to understand precisely what such policies mean.

Urban Open Space

The trend against 'greenfield' development which was a feature of planning policy throughout the 1980s has perforce obliged developers, when looking at undeveloped sites, to consider pockets of open land *within* urban areas. Obvious examples are private sports grounds, surplus schools and school playing fields and extensive back gardens.

Local planning authorities and indeed Government policy have encouraged development of these sites under the name of 'intensification'. The Essex Structure Plan for example relies upon this concept for the provision of over 6500 dwellings in the County between 1977 and 1991.

Such a move is now provoking a reaction from urban planning

authorities who are concerned at the adverse effects of intensification, such as changing the character of an area from one of leafy suburbia to flatland, the loss of 'green lungs' and so on. In Greater London this trend had developed earlier, doubtless because the Green Belt has been longer established round the metropolis. Thus the Greater London Development Plan has an Urban Open Space policy which identifies in diagrammatic form important open spaces which are subject to a policy restraining development on them.

The issue of preserving open spaces in towns came to the fore in June 1989 with discussions in Parliament. Subsequently, a revised Planning Policy Guidance Note on sport and recreation was published in draft in 1990; this stresses the importance of retaining valuable amenity open spaces in towns, such as parks, playing fields, allotments and even private gardens. In planning terms the ability to develop urban open spaces is thus becoming more difficult. The factors which should be taken into account in any evaluation of an open space include the following.

Ownership/existing usage — is the space open to the public? Normally such spaces will be in the ownership of the local authority, as public parks, or school playing fields, where joint usage is operated by the education authority.

Private sports facilities are by definition likely to be unavailable to the general public; the loss of a private facility may therefore be less objectionable since it can be argued that the public (whom planning is meant to protect) has no use of the facility anyway.

Usage of an open space is not the only criterion of its importance; its value may lie in the fact that it is visible as an open space to passers by. Some London squares which are for local residents' use only undoubtedly contribute to the character of the area which the public at large can enjoy and value.

Another factor to be taken into account is the advantage which may accrue to the public if part of a private open space is handed over to the local authority for public use in exchange for some development on the remainder of the open space. This can represent a sensible solution in the case of redundant sports grounds since the owners will not hand them over for public use without some form of gain. For local authorities to propose policies which simply prevent any development on such grounds may be unrealistic and beneficial to no one; indeed it can only point in one direction, namely, compulsory acquisition.

A couple of examples, from Reading and Hertford, will illustrate the above points. The Reading site is a redundant company sports ground some 12 acres (4.8 ha) in extent. The owner wishes to develop it for housing; the Local Authority have a Local Plan for the area which specifically proposes that open spaces in the area should remain open. Since the land is not public it has no value in its existing use other than perhaps as an amenity.

The area in which the ground is situated is deficient in open space. The first stage was to find out the extent of this deficiency. This necessitated defining the relevant area of the town. Clear boundaries such as main roads, a railway line and so on were used because people should not have to cross such boundaries to reach an open space from their homes. The 1981 population of the area was calculated from Small Area Statistics of the Census and the open space standard of the National Playing Fields Association, that is, 2.4 ha per 1 000 population (6 acres/1000 population) was applied. A shortage in the area resulted.

If the site was developed for housing then to meet the open space requirement from the new development it would be necessary to provide 0.8 ha (2 acres) of open space with the remaining 4 ha (10 acres) being given over to housing. In recognition of the shortage of open space in the area and the Local Plan policy to retain private sports grounds the proposed scheme involved double the normal requirement of open space, amounting to 1.6 ha (4 acres) with 3.2 ha (8 acres) for housing. The scheme was, however, rejected by the Council and on the grounds that more of the site should have been kept open. The developer did not pursue the scheme any further because the housing market collapsed in the meantime and the developer could have incurred substantial losses if he had tried to put into effect a modified permission.

In the Hertford case, Structure and Local Plan policies oppose the loss of open spaces in towns especially where they involve recreation uses. The site in question is an area of urban land partly disused and partly occupied by a private sports ground, still in use. Adjoining the sports ground is a primary school which has no playing field of its own. The site owners submitted a scheme to the Local Authority which comprised housing on part of the site, open space and a playing field to be dedicated to the school. An alternative sports ground was proposed some miles away to deal with the relevant Local Plan policy. These proposals clearly sought to address planning policies affecting the site but were nevertheless rejected by the Council and the applicants lodged an appeal, the outcome of which is not known.

Of particular importance in the Hertford scheme is the fact that none of the land is open to the public at present and the proposals would provide a) open space for public use and b) a playing field for the school.

Conservation Areas

Many parts of the built-up areas of the country are designated as Conservation Areas. Section 277 of the 1990 Town and Country Planning Act describes these as: areas of special architectural or historic interest the character or appearance of which it is desirable to preserve or enhance.

The idea of Conservation Areas was first formulated in the 1967 Civic Amenities Act. This Act reflected popular concern to protect the character of attractive towns and villages. Often a village might contain no buildings that individually merited listing but it still had a pleasant character that perhaps derived from a harmony of styles, a pleasing disposition of open spaces and trees between houses, or whatever. The intention of designating a Conservation Area is not therefore, to protect a specific building but the character of the area as a whole, a difference which is not always appreciated by those who operate the system relating to Conservation Areas.

To explain the difference in crude terms: whereas there is a strong presumption against knocking down a listed building, in a Conservation Area it may be possible to knock a building down without spoiling the character of the area; this would obviously apply if the building in question was an eyesore. In addition, Conservation Area status does not mean that building on open spaces in the area is prevented. The correct test to apply is whether a building proposal would 'preserve and enhance' the character of the Area. Even if it did not there might be other factors, for example, removal of a non-conforming use, improvement of highway safety, which could override the fact that the proposal did not preserve or enhance the character of the Area.

In England and Wales alone there were no less than 6 000 Conservation Areas in 1989. As a specific example the Vale of White Horse Rural Area, in Oxfordshire, lists no less than 41 Conservation Areas in villages throughout the area.

It is not difficult to guess where certain areas are likely to be Conservation Areas, for example, the centre of York or Bath. However, there are occasions where the Conservation Area may embrace substantial areas of mundane townscape or buildings which arguably have little architectural/civic design interest. Hertford Conservation Area for example, encompasses much of the town and numerous post-war buildings of little, if any, architectural design interest.

Conservation Areas may also include undeveloped land on the edge of a town or village; they need not be tightly restricted to built-up areas. This is because the character of an area may depend as much on open space between or adjoining buildings as on the buildings themselves. Village greens are a good example. It follows that a vacant site on the edge of a village may not be an automatic candidate for development if the planners have included it in a Conservation Area because it contributes to the character of the Area. It is relatively easy to find out if this is the case or not.

Listed Buildings

A development site may include a listed building, that is to say, a building which the Department of Environment have listed as being of special architectural or historical interest. The effect of listing is to create a presumption against development which results in their demolition or spoils the appearance or setting of the building.

The lists are compiled by the Department of Environment but local authorities keep a copy of the lists for their particular area. The list will indicate the name of the building together with a brief historical/architectural description of it. The description of the listing may refer to various outbuildings and if so these are treated as also being listed. The list distinguishes three grades of building: Grade I — buildings of national importance; Grade II — buildings that are locally important; Grade II * — buildings that are locally important and have internal features of particular merit.

It is very important to check what land around the building is also listed. This may involve looking at the site and forming a view as to the extent of the curtilage of the building, which is not always as simple as it may sound. For example, a farmhouse may be listed but it may not be evident how much of the farmyard should be included as the curtilage of the farmhouse.

The listing of a building obviously represents an obstacle to development of land around or alongside it, but it is not an embargo on development. There are many examples of developments which have involved extensions to listed buildings or new building within the grounds of the listed building.

The criterion which will be taken into account in evaluating a proposal affecting a listed building is the effect which the proposal has on the character of the building. The fact that an extension may alter the character of the building does not rule it out; the question is will the effect be detrimental? This is a matter of subjective, albeit informed, judgement. In practice it is likely that an extension will take the form of a slavish (or faithful depending on your point of view) imitation of the style of the existing building; or it will be an unashamedly modern extension which, however, respects the scale of the existing building. The use of sympathetic materials and appropriate scale for the design will always be important.

The setting of a listed building may also have potential for development and a similar criterion to that outlined above will apply.

Although there are strict controls on development affecting a listed building there is a compensating factor. Government is anxious to preserve listed buildings which form an important part of the nation's heritage. Many of them need urgent attention and repairs but these are invariably very expensive. On occasions a local authority may view sympathetically development proposals which help to restore and assure the future of a listed building by means of the money that is generated by the development.

Sites of Special Scientific Interest

Sites of Special Scientific Interest are designated under the Wildlife and Countryside Act (1891). The authority responsible for designation is the Nature Conservancy Council. Designation indicates that the site is of particular interest from a wildlife point of view. The site could for example contain a rare species of flower or a particular wild animal may frequent the site. Wetlands and heathlands are often designated as SSSIs, reflecting their rapid disappearance in recent decades and the need to protect them as valuable wildlife habitats.

The effect of designation is virtually to prevent any significant development and in this respect they are more restrictive than Green Belts. They are also nearly as extensive as Green Belts, covering 1.46 million ha and numbering 4 846 in 1989.

Scheduled Ancient Monuments

In 1984 there were about 12 800 monuments in England alone which had been scheduled under the Ancient Monuments and Archaeological Areas Act 1979. The effect of this scheduling is to protect the monuments from any operations which might damage them, unless the prior consent of the Department of the Environment had been obtained.

In looking at a site it may not be obvious that it is an ancient monument. The value of the site may be entirely hidden with little if any sign of it on the surface. However, it is possible to find out whether a site is scheduled by consulting the county or district council for the area or by undertaking a legal search. The owner of the land in question will have been notified by the Department of the Environment at the time the site was designated an ancient monument.

The effect of scheduling does not necessarily prevent development. It is only in very rare cases involving monuments of national importance, that English Heritage (who advise the Department of the Environment) would normally recommend an absolute embargo on development. More often they require the developer to carry out an archaeological dig, first of all to establish the extent of the monument and secondly to excavate it, recording and preserving whatever finds are of value. The act of excavation is likely to be 'destructive' in the sense that it destroys the original setting of the monument. The monument may well be reconstructed in a nearby museum.

Excavation is an expensive process and it may cost tens of thousands of pounds. Only a major development proposal would warrant such outlay and the developer may quickly abort a proposal if he discovers that the site is an ancient monument.

Agricultural Land Quality

The agricultural quality of a site is an important factor in evaluating its development potential. Clearly it is not a factor that applies in built up areas; what is perhaps less obvious is that it does not apply to woodland areas in the countryside. Nor, for example, does it apply to disused airfields. These are examples of a number of uses which are broadly described as non-agricultural. Other uses are golf courses, sports fields and private parkland.

The quality of land throughout England and Wales has been surveyed by the Ministry of Agriculture, Fisheries and Food and their findings are set out in a series of coloured maps covering England and Wales. These are published at two main scales, 1:250 000 and 1: 63 360. The former provides information of sub-regional importance which is unlikely to be of value in evaluating specific development sites; the more commonly used maps are those at 1:63 360 scale, but even these are not wholly reliable. They show areas in broad-brush rather than fine detail; thus an area of up to 80 ha of top quality land within an area of average quality land would not show up on the Ministry's map.

In October 1988 the Ministry of Agriculture published new guidelines on how it defined agricultural land quality. These guidelines came into effect at the beginning of 1989. They follow previous guidelines in so far as they grade agricultural land in a series of descending grades, with Grade 1 being the very best farmland in the country and Grade 5 being the very worst. Appendix 2 lists the different grades with their main characteristics.

About one-third of agricultural land in England and Wales consists of Grade 1 and Grade 2 and 3a land; almost one half is Grade 3b or Grade 4.

Government policy, as expressed in Department of the Environment Circular 16/87 and reiterated in structure plans up and down the country, is that the best agricultural land should not be used for development if lower grade agricultural land could be used instead. The agricultural quality of a site is therefore a very important factor when evaluating its potential for development.

In recent years there has been considerable debate about the need to retain every last acre or hectare of agricultural land because of the surpluses in food production that have developed, particularly in the European Community. Since 1987 there has been greater emphasis on retaining agricultural land for its own sake rather than for its productive ability. In other words the environmental and planning aspects of open countryside assumed greater importance. The effect of this change in Department policy is that a site which is of average agricultural quality may now be more difficult to achieve development on, if it serves an important environmental purpose. Conversely, good quality farmland that does not serve a planning purpose may be more vulnerable to development.

Mineral-bearing Land

Planning is concerned to make the best use of natural resources of which minerals is a prime example. Many structure and local plans contain specific policies designed to ensure that deposits of sand, gravel, ballstone, chalk, limestone, etc. are not built over. It does not follow that areas containing such deposits are incapable of being development sites. Many authorities are prepared to accept development in such areas (subject to other planning considerations) provided that the developer first extracts the minerals from the land which he wishes to develop.

While this general approach may sound straightforward, in practice there can be a number of complicating factors. For example, mineral-bearing land may adjoin an area of housing. The land is suitable for housing development, as an extension of the housing area, but the public authority is anxious that the minerals should be extracted first. The operation of taking out the minerals will result in noise, dust and traffic, all to the detriment of the adjoining housing. Should the local authority sacrifice the minerals in order to preserve residential amenity, or vice versa? There is no simple answer. Furthermore, it may be that the removal of the minerals, resulting in a lowering of ground levels, could well result in an unsatisfactory relationship with adjoining housing on higher ground.

Open-cast coal mining may cause similar environmental concerns as sand and gravel extraction. Unless it is properly restored a site will end up an eyesore. Also the ground must be properly compacted after the coal has been taken out, if it is then to be suitable for development. In some cases a site may be unsuitable for development by reason of previous underground workings. Open-cast mining of the site could be advantageous for the reasons: a) it renders the site physically developable; b) the resultant site is more suitable for development from a town planning point of view.

In areas where open-cast coal mining occurs it is important to check whether a site contains coal deposits and what the local plan for the area says. Thus, at Garforth, north east of Leeds, the local plan has a specific policy that prohibits open-cast mining in certain specified areas because of its effect on the local environment.

Another issue relating to mineral land is whether the land is actually worth working. The economics of extraction may be such that a site is not worth extracting because there is insufficient mineral to interest an operator, particularly if the mineral, say gravel, has to be washed and graded with expensive plant in order to command a worthwhile price. In these circumstances is the safeguarding policy of the local authority justified?

Although the above factors complicate the issue, arguably they should not inhibit the planning authority from devising specific mineral policies which they will then have to balance against other policies, for example protection of amenity, when they receive a planning application. The local authority is bound to survey its area for minerals, map the relevant deposits and devise appropriate policies to safeguard those deposits.

A good example is Berkshire where the Planning Authority has prepared a Minerals Subject Plan and listed different categories of 'prospect area', reflecting the need to balance the requirements of the construction industry with other planning factors. The subject plan identifies three categories of mineral bearing land where extraction is encouraged or discouraged in varying degrees. These are: a) Areas of Maximum Objection, b) Restricted Areas and c) Prospect Areas. The first are areas which are subject to major constraints and where planning permission for mineral extraction is very unlikely to be forthcoming; Restricted Areas are areas of some restriction where planning permission may be granted if there are exceptional circum-stances; Prospect Areas are all mineral-bearing areas not subject to the restrictions in categories a and b.

Plan 8 shows an extract from the plan covering the area south of Reading. The effect of the policy on development sites would appear to be as follows. Where a proposal is on mineral-bearing land whose extraction would attract maximum objection, then the fact that the development would sterilise the deposit probably does not count against it. If a development proposal is on land in a Prospect Area it would be resisted by the Council because the development would sterilise the deposit. A means of overcoming such an objection would be to extract the minerals and then carry out the development, but anyone contemplating such an exercise would need to weigh up the value of the mineral deposit and the additional cost of having to build on what would probably be made-up ground.

Floodland

Local river authorities have designated areas that lie within the floodplain of rivers for which they are responsible. Within these areas

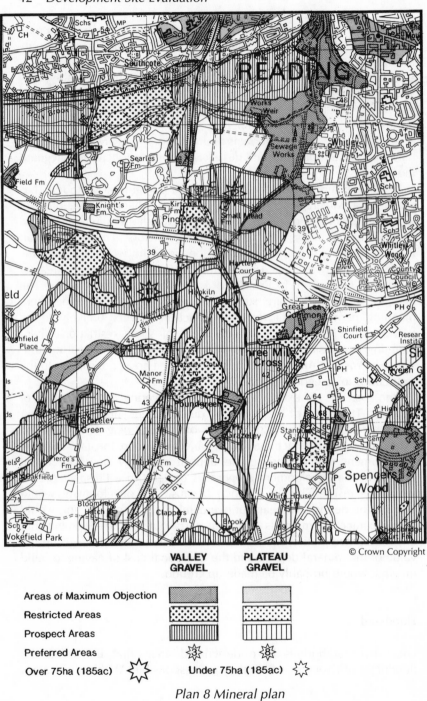

© Crown Copyright

	VALLEY GRAVEL	PLATEAU GRAVEL
Areas of Maximum Objection		
Restricted Areas		
Prospect Areas		
Preferred Areas		
Over 75ha (185ac) ☆	☆3	☆8
	Under 75ha (185ac) ☆	

Plan 8 Mineral plan

any development proposals which involve buildings, whether occupied or not, are likely to attract a strong objection from the river authority. The planning authority are not bound to stand by such an objection but it is likely that they will do so unless there are very strong reasons otherwise.

It is possible to find out whether land is within a floodplain by consulting the river authority for the area. The authority holds maps which define the floodplains. Although it may appear straightforward to find out if land is liable to flood or not, two factors should be borne in mind. First, is the map out of date? There may have been improvements to the river system since the map was drawn up which result in a redefinition of the floodplain. Second, it may be possible to develop land in the floodplain if adequate compensation works are undertaken. Thus a scheme which occupied 1 ha of land that lay 1 metre below the flood level could become acceptable if a) the land was built up by a metre, and b) a compensating volume of land, previously not in the floodplain was scooped out. This land would then compensate, in flooding terms, for the land to be developed.

Safeguarding Zones

These are areas, normally adjacent to airports, where development is strictly controlled. They comprise areas beyond either end of a runway where there is a risk of a plane crash on take-off or landing. The local plan for the area in which the airport is situated indicates the extent of the safeguarding zones. For example, there are safeguarding zones round Heathrow Airport which are shown in the Spelthorne Local Plan. In a safeguarding zone some development may be possible, for example car parking or open storage, so long as it does not involve the regular presence of people in the zone.

Safeguarding zones are normally, but not exclusively, associated with airports. At Avonmouth by the Bristol Channel the area surrounding the chemical works is designated a safeguarding zone within which new housing is not permitted, because of the risk to residents in the event of an accident at the works. This safeguarding zone does not preclude other industrial development.

Non-spatial Constraints

The foregoing paragraphs have dealt with planning constraints that have a geographical or spatial basis. They may cover an area, for example an Area of Outstanding Natural Beauty or a site, for example a listed building. To complete the picture we need to look at non-spatial constraints. These can often have an important bearing on the conclusion that we come to when evaluating a site. Such constraints represent a layer of planning policy which is often to be found in local planning documents.

Car Parking

The need to provide car parking within a development site is likely to determine the amount of development that can occur on the site. Standards for car parking vary from one local authority to another and they also vary according to the type of development. Housing for example may need to have two parking spaces for every house; an office block may have to provide one space for every 20 m² of office space.

In some larger towns the amount of parking on site is actively discouraged, because of the problems which could arise from a large number of uncontrolled private car parks in the centre. Yet the provision of parking within office development is one of the most important factors affecting their marketability. Therefore, it is essential to find out at the evaluation stage what level of parking can be achieved within the policies of the planning authority.

Environmental Standards

Environmental standards may have been drawn up by the planning authority and these should be taken into account in evaluating the potential of a site. Typically these relate to the density of acceptable development, the amount of daylighting to be preserved round buildings and the size of back gardens.

In Barnet for example the Council drew up standards in 1988, endorsing previous standards, which covered such matters as density for houses; overlooking between dwellings; sunlight, daylight, noise; amount of amenity space per dwelling; car parking provision; refuse collection; and landscaping.

The application of these standards to a specific proposal can be seen in a planning application for 50 flats at a site in Barnet. The application was approved in 1989 and the flats have been built. When the application was ready to go to committee the Planning Officer evaluated it in the following way:

> The land has an area of 0.85 ha and the development would have 150 habitable rooms giving a density of 176 habitable rooms per hectare. This would accord with the relevant density standards. Parking is provided in accordance with Council standard of 1.3 spaces per unit.

> The flats were 25–27 m from the boundaries of adjoining properties which minimises overlooking problems. The rear garden would provide the equivalent of 72 m^2 of amenity space per flat.

In evaluating greenfield development sites the developer and planning authority will need to have regard to the policy for settlement planning. Although most local authorities draw up their own settlement policies they usually share many features in common and reflect national policy guidance, such as is set out in Planning Policy Guidance Notes Nos. 1 and 3. First of all there is a presumption against development in open countryside, unrelated to existing settlements. Therefore a site is unlikely to have much development potential if it is half a mile from the nearest town or village. Exceptions to this general principle do arise. A site previously used as a defence establishment or having redundant buildings on it might be considered suitable for new development even if it was isolated. The planning authority might even welcome the relocation of 'non-conforming' or unneighbourly use to such a site.

The other main exception is a new settlement proposal. Several proposals for major development in open countryside have been put forward by developers in the period 1986–90. Although none has been approved at the time of writing there are sufficient indications from the Government, for example in draft Planning Policy Guidance Note No. 3 that the concept is not outside the realms of possibility. The Note states that indeed new settlements are not unprecedented. There is a respectable pedigree of such schemes from such early examples as New Lanark in the nineteenth century and the New Towns of the 1950s onwards.

The possibility of a site being suitable for a new settlement will require at the very least a strong statistical basis showing the need for additional housing, and all the other elements of the planning balance (loss of farm land, etc.) will need to be taken into account.

Apart from the above exceptions, planning policy opposes development away from cities, towns and villages and prefers development on infill sites on land previously developed or, as a second best, on the edge of existing settlements. Infill sites have provided a good source of supply for new development, albeit in the late 1980s a strong body of opinion has emerged which resists the use of such sites because their development may detract from the openness of an area, may cause overlooking, or access problems, and so on.

In the case of previously developed land the principle of development is unlikely to be at stake and consideration will centre on various details; with regard to peripheral development the planners and developer will wish to consider how well related the site is to the settlement. Does it have only one boundary abutting existing buildings, or is there development on several sides already? Secondly, is the site of a scale that is appropriate to the settlement? A 4-ha (10-acre) field might have several boundaries adjoining a small village, but because of its size its development for housing could be out of scale with the number of houses in the village.

While it is a relatively easy matter to ascertain whether a site or property is affected by a particular planning constraint and one can make a judgement as to whether the site is well related to an existing settlement, it is not so easy to judge how important a constraint is to the development of the site. As we have seen, the fact that a site may fall within an Area of Outstanding Natural Beauty need not rule out the possibility of development on it. However, local authorities often reject proposals on the grounds that they fall within such an area.

There is no simple rule as to whether a particular planning constraint should override development. Rather there is first of all a gradation of severity of individual constraints and secondly there is a balancing process, as between the severity of one or more constraints and the desirability of a particular proposal. Thus, taking the first aspect, the Green Belt constraint arguably represents the most severe in the continuum, whilst Grade III B agricultural land may not be a particularly severe objection.

By way of example, an Inspector from the Department of the Environment considered a proposal for 6 houses on the edge of Haywards Heath in 1990. The local authority had rejected the proposal on various grounds including effect on road safety. The applications appealed and the Inspector dismissed the appeal. However, he commented:

> In respect of highway conditions ... provided that road and access proposals meet standards for a built-up area, it would in my view, be unreasonable to oppose the development of the site on highway grounds.

In addition he felt that limited weight should be given to the existing local plans for the area. But he felt that the effect of the scheme on the open countryside was unacceptable and this weighed more heavily than the previous factors.

Looking at the second aspect, namely the balancing process, the desirability of a superstore, bringing investment and employment to an area and reducing a perceived deficiency in provision, might outweigh a recreation policy objection which required part of the site to remain as a sports field.

On the other hand, taking the example from Hertford already referred to, owners of a 6 ha site in the town proposed housing and open space on land comprising unused land and a sports ground. In putting his report to the Planning Committee the Planning Officer stated:

> It is accepted that there are certain advantages to be gained from the development. However, these do not override the Local Plan presumptions against the development of most of the site.

It is evident that the balancing process is often a matter of judgement and opinion and no amount of analysis will indicate for sure which way the balance will tip.

The appraisal of planning policies and constraints is an essential part of development site evaluation. It can also be used in searching for development sites through what is called sieve analysis. This technique simply overlays the mappable planning constraints on a map, to build up a composite picture of the area. Those parts of the area which are subject to least constraint are the areas where development sites are most likely to be found. This technique is widely used by local authorities and developers, the former in their task of finding the most suitable land for development needs, and the latter in seeking out sites that have the best chance of getting planning permission. Plan 9 is an example of a simple sieve analysis of part of Devon carried out for a housebuilding company.

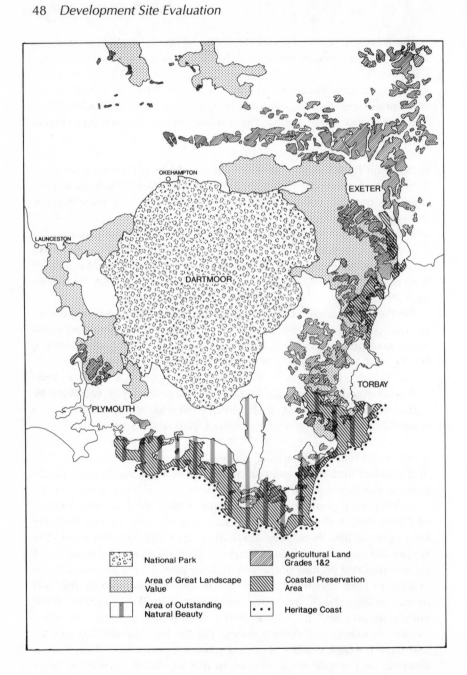

Plan 9 Sieve analysis

The analysis shows the extent of the several planning constraints. White areas are those subject to none of the above constraints and therefore have more promise for development. Such an analysis often duplicates the local authority's own plan for the area, but it can be refined so as to take account of a developer's particular objectives. Thus an oil company might overlay a simple sieve map with a plan of main roads and the location of existing filling stations in order to determine whether an area of the sieve map was appropriate for a new garage, commercially, as well as from a town planning standpoint.

The technique is of little use when looking at areas that have already been built on. In these cases there is likely to be little doubt about the planning principle of redevelopment; the planning arguments will be about the amount and nature of the redevelopment.

Within a built-up area there will be existing buildings which are potential development sites. The planning considerations which apply to such sites are different from those that apply to edge-of-town or greenfield sites.

The amount or density of development that can be achieved on the site will often depend on the density of adjoining development, but there may be scope to achieve a higher density, if the development extends further back from the frontage than adjoining development, or if more storeys can be achieved within a given height. In some areas the planning authority will have a set standard of density, expressed as a plot ratio, whereby the floorspace of new development must not exceed a certain multiple of the area of the plot. The plot area is traditionally taken to include half the width of any roads which adjoin it.

Other technical standards which the local authority may apply are parking provision and sunlight and daylight indicators. These standards may influence the amount of development that can be achieved on a site; thus it may be necessary to set aside a substantial area of the site for car parking in accordance with the council's standards, or it may be possible to 'commute' the parking. This involves making a payment (which by law should be a voluntary payment) in lieu of each parking space that is not provided on site. The payment is made to the local authority and should be used by them towards the provision of car parking in their area.

Sunlight and daylight are more important to residential than commercial development, but the local authority may insist that a building is stepped back on upper levels to enable adequate daylight to other buildings.

Reference has already been made to Conservation Areas and listed buildings. In a built-up area Conservation Area status may mean that the facades of existing buildings have to be retained in any redevelopment proposals, which could seriously limit the amount of floorspace that can be created in a new development. Where there are listed buildings, the developer must assume that permission is unlikely to be forthcoming for their demolition and any development proposals will be limited to refurbishment and rearrangement of accommodation within the existing structure of the building. The fact that a building is listed, though, does not mean that extensions to it will be ruled out of court.

4 Site Factors

In this chapter we shall consider a number of physical factors affecting the development potential of land and buildings. These are in contrast to the planning factors considered previously which are in the nature of policy constraints.

Access

Access is one of the most obvious yet frequently neglected essentials of a development site. In most cases vehicular access is necessary; in a few cases pedestrian access only is needed. Redevelopment of a shop or office in a town centre could, for example, be feasible without vehicular access, on the basis that there was no on-site parking and deliveries were made by trolley or similar means. Clearly this represents the exception rather than the rule. Even in a town centre a new development will normally require vehicular access for delivery vehicles even though cars may be unable to reach the development. Outside town centres access is required both for deliveries, employees or customers and visitors; in the case of housing the need is obvious.

When evaluating a site for development one of the first questions to ask is, 'Can access be obtained?' 'Access' hereafter is taken to mean vehicular access. In answering this question it is necessary to look at the title plans relating to the site. If they show that the site abuts a highway there should be no problem. A highway is a road over which the public has a right of way and that includes the developer of the site. He is entitled to bring vehicles to his site from the highway.

What is the highway? It is relatively easy to find out the extent of a highway if it has been adopted by the highway authority. There will normally be a plan at the council offices which the public can consult and from which they may find out the extent of the highway. This may include not only the carriageway of a road but also footpaths, verges and adjoining land, possibly extending to several metres either side of the road. On occasions it will not be obvious just how far a highway extends, either because there is no clear plan at the council offices or because the road has not been adopted by the council. If a road is unadopted it will be necessary to look on the ground and see if the extent of the road is obvious. If it is not, problems arise. Let us assume for one moment that the extent of the road is fairly apparent. If the road is not adopted, this means quite simply that the responsibility for its upkeep lies with the property owners either side of the road. It does not mean that the road is private and that an individual is not allowed to drive over it. However, it does mean that an individual can only improve or alter the road with the agreement of the adjoining property owners.

Moving down in the scale of accessibility is a site or building to which access can be obtained only via a private road. There is not even a right of access in this case, let alone a right to improve the road.

Finally, there is the site which does not adjoin a road at all, of whatever status. In this case other land lies between the site and a road, and no access is possible without the agreement of the owner of the intervening land.

The ways of overcoming this problem are considered later in the chapter, but before leaving the question of access we need to widen the definition of what access entails. It may mean rather more than simply a dropped kerb off a carriageway with a suitable width of frontage to enable the construction of the side road or driveway into the site. There must be adequate visibility at the entrance to a site so that drivers can enter and leave the site safely. Standards of required visibility vary, according to the nature of the development proposed on the site and the type of road from which the site takes access. There is a world of difference between the visibility requirements of a single house with its driveway off a cul-de-sac and those of a business park adjoining a dual carriageway.

The significance of these requirements is that a developer must demonstrate to the highway authority that he can achieve the necessary visibility if he wishes to get planning permission for his proposal. The proposed access to a site requires visibility to right and left and the area within which such visibility must be achieved is defined by the triangles ABC and BCD. AC and CD are called 'sight lines' and their position depends on the major and minor road distances indicated on the plan. Useful guidance on these distances can be found in Planning Policy Guidance Note No. 13, Appendix C.

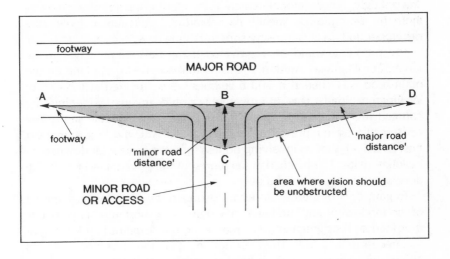

Plan 10 T-junction

The minor road distance for a new junction is normally 9 m; this may sometimes be reduced to 4.5 m or even 2.4 m. The major road distance varies according to the speed of traffic on the major road and is likely to fall between 70 m and 120 m on many occasions, although the extremes vary from about 30 m to 300 m.

Within the triangles ABC and BCD there must be no obstruction of visibility in either direction. This triangle of visibility only applies above 1 m above ground level. A low-growing bush or a roadside bench would not be regarded as an obstruction if they were less than 1 m in height, the assumption being that the driver of a car can see over objects of less than 1 m.

Plan 11 shows the practical effect of the visibility requirement. It is based on a site in Essex. The site is at the end of a road known as Wellington Road. Wellington Road meets the main road (Hockley Road) at a T-junction. The view of the Highway Authority on the development site is that visibility splays, depicted by triangles ABC (hatched) and BCD, are required if about ten houses are built. The two triangles primarily affect land in the highway, but part of triangle ABC cuts across the front gardens of nos. 214 and 216 and part of triangle BCD (also hatched) affects nos. 222 and 224. Although the garden does not obstruct visibility at present, there is nothing to stop the owner planting a hedge or trees or building a wall, which could obstruct visibility.

Accordingly, the developer must ensure that he has control over this land; for example, by means of a binding agreement between the developer and owners and any subsequent owners.

The problem would be aggravated if the development was to be larger. The Highway Authority insisted that a right-turning lane on the main road was needed if 100 dwellings were provided at the end of Wellington Road. This improvement would involve widening the carriageway and putting splays further back onto private land. The revised splays are represented by the triangles ABE and BDE and affect nos. 212–230, that is, involving no less than ten private landowners to negotiate with. The hatched areas represent the private land which the developer must gain control over.

To gain control the developer must obtain the necessary agreement of the landowner and the latter may demand a substantial payment as the price of his agreement. He may even refuse point blank to grant the necessary control. There is nothing that the developer can do about this. Unless he is a body vested with statutory powers of compulsory acquisition, he cannot force an unwilling vendor to sell. Can he ask the highway or planning authority, who do have statutory powers of compulsory acquisition, to acquire the land on his behalf? The answer is nearly always no. This is because public authorities do not see it as their role to facilitate development solely for the benefit of the developer. If there was a clear public benefit arising from the development a public authority might lend its weight to compulsory acquisition.

An example would be a town centre redevelopment scheme involving multiple land ownership which the local authority had included in an approved local plan. In such a situation the local authority might help the developer to acquire property if it was necessary beyond doubt to enable the scheme to proceed. If there is no public benefit the developer cannot expect much, if any, support from the local authority to acquire land, a point which is worth remembering if there is any doubt as to the ability to provide access.

Ground Conditions

In most cases it will be necessary to examine carefully the ground conditions of a site, whether it is virgin land or previously developed. There are several aspects to look at under the general heading of ground conditions. First of all, the subsoil must be stable for building

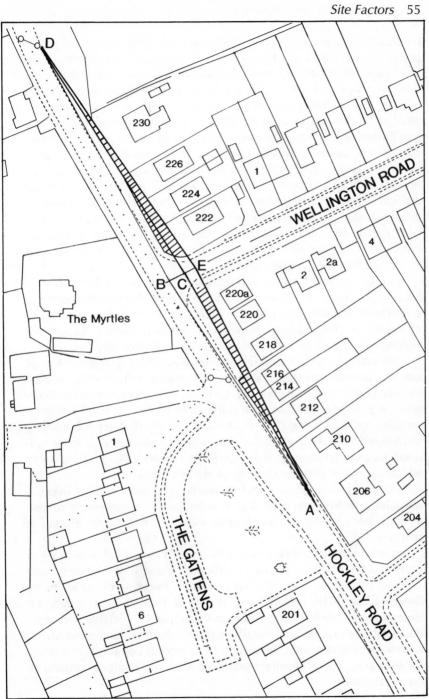

Plan 11 Sight lines

© Crown Copyright

purposes. Where for example there are layers of sand and gravel below the top soil it will be necessary to obtain a bearing from firmer soil below. Alternatively, it may be possible to design special foundations such as rafts with a lesser bearing requirement. There is a variety of technical solutions to unstable ground conditions whether by rafts, piles or whatever. Although the type of subsoil may not therefore be fundamental to the site appraisal, it has a very obvious cost implication for any development proposals and should be investigated as a matter of course at the outset of any evaluation. Occasions where such an investigation is not essential might include land previously built on or a pocket of land, surrounded by housing, which is itself proposed for 2-storey housing. As a general rule one should always obtain a geological survey of a site from qualified engineers who will dig a series of boreholes and take samples to identify the character of the subsoils and ascertain their load bearing capacities.

At either extreme are rock and peat, the former being able to sustain bearing pressures of 1 000–4 000 kN/m^2 whilst peat is not considered suitable for any substantial form of building. There are four main types of subsoil — rock subsoil (sandstone, limestone, chalk, etc.), non-cohesive soils (gravel), cohesive soils (clay) and silt or silty clay.

Clay subsoil can be problematic because in very dry weather it shrinks, producing large cracks in the ground which may weaken foundations. In wet weather, by contrast, clay does not drain freely and it may hold a lot of water. It is therefore liable to expand and exert pressure on foundations. If a site is being considered for housing development and it overlaps a clay subsoil then the developer will need to take account of the additional cost of deeper foundations which are not affected by clay shrinkage or expansion.

Sand and gravel, often found as layers in areas of alluvial deposit, have little bearing strength and it will always be necessary to pile through such layers at considerable expense until firmer ground is reached.

A more serious situation arises if the ground is unsuitable because of underground cavities, slopes or ground compression. Underground cavities may arise naturally, for example because of rocks being dissolved away by underground water; or from human action, for example, coal mining. Sloping ground also may be unstable and again the instability may occur naturally or be the result of human endeavour such as an embankment. Instability from ground compression occurs, for example, where development takes place on made-up ground or on alluvial soils.

It is normally the responsibility of the developer to assess whether a site is unstable or not but local planning authorities should also bear it in mind when they consider the allocation of land for development. Planning Policy Guidance Note No. 14, dealing with development on unstable land makes this very clear:

> It is important that the stability of the ground is considered at all stages of the planning process...In preparing and altering their development plans local authorities need to take into account the possibility of ground instability. Development plans provide an opportunity to set out policies for the reclamation and use of unstable land.
>
> (paragraph 24, 25)

The Note includes technical appendices on ground instability including sources of information on the subject.

Drainage

The geological survey can also be useful in determining the prevailing water table. Where the water table lies only a few feet below the surface of a site the construction of foundations on the site will be hampered by the constant need to pump water away. However, it should be remembered that the provision of a surface water drainage system can, in itself, lower the water table of a site. This could be important on a low lying site with a high water table. The geological survey should also assist in determining how surface water can be drained from a site following its development. Again, this is a technical matter which can usually be resolved but it can have a significant cost implication. Thus the provision of surface water soakaways which convey surface water a short distance from buildings and allow it to percolate naturally into the subsoil is a much cheaper solution than having to construct a new surface water sewer possibly several hundred metres long. A new sewer may connect into the existing surface water sewer network but on occasions this may not be necessary. An alternative solution, where the conditions are right, is to connect a new surface water sewer to an existing watercourse such as a river or stream. The feasibility of this will depend on how far away the water course is and whether its capacity will accept an additional flow. If the capacity is too small one solution may be to construct a 'balancing pond' which retains surface water from the development during periods of heavy rain and releases the surface water into the watercourse during dry weather.

It may well be possible to dispense with a geological survey when determining how surface water can be disposed of. In a built-up area the likelihood is that there will be surface water sewers or combined sewers near the site and drainage will be by means of a connection to the nearest main sewer.

As part of the initial evaluation of a site the developer should check with the drainage authority whether there is a surface water sewer and if so, where and what size it is. There may be a sewer nearby, but of inadequate size for the additional discharge created by the development. Depending on the advice of the developer's engineer this might necessitate replacing the sewer with a larger one or possibly 'balancing' the extra run-off from the site via a balancing pond or larger on-site sewer. The intention of either solution is to ensure that the amount of run-off from the development does not exceed the amount prior to the development, when it actually reaches the main sewer.

In the rural situation or semi-rural situation, particularly in the case of housing schemes, surface water may be drained to soakaways but local authorities often insist that the run-off from roads is to a sewer rather than soakaway because of possible spillage onto roads which should not be allowed to percolate into the subsoil.

Foul drainage must normally be to a sewer. Exceptions are in rural small-scale development. In the case of larger schemes a private sewage treatment works may be necessary. These are the exceptions. Generally, the development site will require a foul sewer to drain to and the developer will wish to enquire of the drainage authority at an early stage where the nearest foul sewer is. He will also need to know if it is of adequate capacity and likewise in the case of the sewage works to which it connects.

Ideally, the connection to a local authority sewer will enable sewage to flow by gravity. Where this is not possible it will be necessary for the developer to pump the sewage up to the sewer. This will involve the cost of providing a pumping station and seeking the agreement (which will only be obtained, if at all, at a price) of the drainage authority to adopt and maintain the pumping station.

Mention has been made of the drainage authority in respect of both surface and foul drainage. It is as well to know which authority is involved. The Water Act 1989 reorganised the administration of drainage, water supply and river management. The relevant drainage authority for an area is now the water company, for example Thames

Water Company, and it is this company or its agents whom the developer must consult. In many towns and cities the local council (district, borough or city council) will have a drainage department and it is they who will advise the developer on the drainage system. The evaluation of a site may reveal that there is no sewer to serve it and the nearest public sewer is some way away. The developer must therefore have a sewer constructed across third-party land. It is important to remember that this does not put the developer at the mercy of the third party. In this respect there is a fundamental difference between sewers and roads. Where vehicular access is not available the developer may well be ransomed by a third party. However, if planning permission has been obtained for what the developer is contemplating, he can 'requisition' or order the water company to construct a sewer to serve the development.

This power is provided by Section 34 of the Public Health Act 1936 and applies to both foul and surface water sewers, serving residential or non-residential development, provided they do not serve only a single dwelling. By definition a sewer serves more than a single dwelling. A further qualification is that the sewer will be constructed to serve 'domestic' waste as opposed to, say, industrial effluent. Domestic waste does however, include waste from both houses and the 'domestic' effluent of factories, offices, etc. Where a developer requisitions a sewer he will be expected to pay for it and obviously this should be taken into account early on when a site is being examined.

In addition the developer of a residential site will have to pay an 'infrastructure charge', regardless of whether his development necessitates a new sewer. This charge was introduced by Section 79 of the Water Act 1989 and, as an example of the amount of charge, the figure in the Wessex Water Company area in 1989 was £983 per dwelling for sewerage and sewage treatment, and £551 per dwelling for water supply. In addition there is a connection, or 'tapping' charge, of £150 per dwelling for water supply. The infrastructure charges will directly affect the value of a development site, but as a small consolation to the developer, it appears that he will no longer be expected to contribute separately to upgrading sewage treatment works. The amount of charge that is levied on non-residential proposals has not been standardised in the way that the charge for residential proposals has and it will be a matter of negotiation.

Finally, it should be noted that the developer may also requisition a supply of water, again provided that it is not to serve a single dwelling.

Contaminated/Filled Ground

As the pressure to develop on previously developed sites continues, there are growing instances of development on contaminated or filled ground. Old gas works, factories, railway land and waste tips are the more common examples. A geological survey is essential in identifying the nature of contamination, its depth and extent and the measures needed to enable development safely to proceed. It is likely that specialist engineers will be required to advise the site owner or developer rather than general site surveyors.

Where the ground is contaminated or filled it may rule out certain types of development on economic grounds. This should be of concern not only to the site owner and developer but also the local authority since there is little point in proposing it for a particular use if the economics of restoration preclude such a use.

Government advice on the development of contaminated land and filled land can be found in Circulars 21/87 and 17/89 published by the Department of the Environment. In the case of the former it is up to the developer to investigate the nature of any contamination and satisfy the local authority that he can successfully deal with any problems posed by it. The local authority will have regard to this when considering the developer's application for planning permission.

Filled land is under growing pressure for redevelopment in order to safeguard open countryside. The danger which Circular 17/89 addresses is principally that of gas being generated from land-fill sites. Detailed technical advice is available from the Department of the Environment as to how build-ups of gas can be avoided. Again, it is the developer's responsibility to demonstrate that his proposals for development deal satisfactorily with any problems of gas generation. The sanction which the local authority has over the developer is that the presence of gas on filled land is a material planning consideration and it is open to the local authority to refuse planning permission if the developer fails to satisfy them on this aspect.

There are other hazards arising from contaminated and filled land, such as instability, and these too must be carefully assessed by expert engineers or surveyors with recommendations on how and at what cost they can be overcome.

The presence of existing buildings on a development site has a number of implications. There is first the cost of removing the buildings and in a densely built-up area this may include the cost of supporting adjoining buildings.

Secondly, are there problems below the ground? The existing buildings may have basement areas that must be filled before redevelopment commences. It is very likely that the foundations of the previous building will be unsuited to the new proposal.

Below ground structures may be so substantial that they cannot be removed economically and the new building has to be designed around them. An extreme example is the Department of the Environment office in Marsham Street London where underground concrete structures erected during the Second World War dictated the distinctive 3-tower design of the present building.

In evaluating a site the prospective developer will wish to carry out a geological survey; it may be that the vendor himself has commissioned a survey and the developer should then request a copy of the survey and results. Provided that independent professionals have carried out the survey the developer should be reasonably confident of its reliability, particularly if he has his own engineer to check the survey methods and interpretation of the results.

In certain areas coal mining has taken place or is still active. If the developer, perhaps through local knowledge or as a result of discussions with the local authority, has reason to believe that a site may be affected by mine workings he should contact the local office of the National Coal Board. They will provide an initial report on payment of a small amount showing the extent of workings and their implications for whether a site can be developed or not. Such a survey is indispensable and can be obtained in a matter of a few weeks. A further report, available to local authorities, is the Mineral Valuers' report which is more detailed than the NCB report. Also, it covers any underground workings not just those undertaken for coal extraction. The report is not normally available to private individuals, but it may be possible to discuss the contents with the authority.

Underground Services/Cables

The main underground services and cables which need to be checked relate to foul and surface water drainage, and the supply of water, electricity, gas, telephone and oil. It is possible to find out whether and where these services run by consulting the various statutory undertakers who are responsible for the service in question. Normally, statutory undertakers try to locate such services in the footpath or pavement alongside a road where access for maintenance and repair causes the least inconvenience. Although this is the normal practice it must be remembered that some services have been in place for decades and one should not take for granted that a site for development will be free of underground services. The British Pipeline Agency will provide information on their equipment which is principally petroleum pipelines. It is often possible to identify the presence of underground lines in rural areas by ground markers or white painted stiles on field boundaries.

The local authority technical services department often keeps Ordnance Survey maps at 1:1 250 or 1:2 500 scale showing where foul and surface water sewers run in their area. The maps are not 100 per cent accurate and they warn that a possible deviation either side of the line shown on the map must be allowed for.

The local office of the Electricity Board likewise keeps maps of underground and overground electricity cables, indicating whether they are high or low tension and what the voltage is. Outside towns and cities it is unlikely that high-voltage cables will be found underground, because of the cost compared to carrying the electricity via overhead pylons. Information on gas and telephone lines is obtainable from the local office of the gas or telephone authority.

The implications for site evaluation of underground services arise in two ways. Where a service such as a foul sewer crosses a site the water authority stipulates that building should not be allowed over the line of the sewer or within 3 m of either side of the line. This is to enable maintenance of the sewer to be carried out easily. Also, it avoids excessive pressure being placed on the sewer from buildings above it. This restriction can be overcome in exceptional circumstances but it will require expensive construction techniques and may require an acceptance of liability by the developer if maintenance works have to be undertaken which affect a building over the sewer.

An alternative may be to divert the sewer. The resultant sewer must be effective though and therefore its alignment and fall must comply with the approved technical standards. Even where this can be achieved the cost of diversion must be weighed in the balance bearing in mind it could range from £150–£300 per metre at 1990 prices. This figure could increase if other services e.g. telephone cables were also affected by the diversion.

In addition, an underground service which adjoins a site may need diverting because of road or other works alongside the site which result from the proposed development. Thus the realignment of a footpath to improve visibility splays into a site may require that telephone cables under the footpath have to be realigned so that they remain under the footpath and do not end up under the carriageway. The latter may be subject to the pressures of heavy lorries which could damage the cables. Diversion of telephone cables can be a very expensive operation.

Overhead Electricity Cables

Overhead cables may appear to be an overriding obstacle to development of a site but this is not the case. There is no reason why buildings, whether offices or houses, should not be built under overhead lines and there are many examples. There is, though, a psychological objection to building houses under overhead lines, and certainly there is some evidence of a possible effect on people who live under electricity lines.

Technically, the only constraint which overhead lines impose is that buildings must be clear of the lines by a certain distance which varies according to the voltage of the lines.

It will sometimes be necessary to divert an overhead line so that a site can be developed without hindrance. The economic consequences can be severe. In the case of major pylons carrying 132 kV or 400 kV lines it may cost a million pounds per pylon to divert a line. Lower voltage lines, on the other hand, for example 11 kV and 33 kV, can be readily moved for a few thousand pounds on a small site.

Telephone Cables

A site investigation may reveal telephone cables that need diverting if a development is to proceed. Normally this is not a problem. However, if the cables are a major part of the network, the developer should at all cost avoid the necessity of moving them, particularly if they are fibre optic cables. These cannot be cut and rejoined in the way that traditional coaxial cables can. It is necessary to relay perhaps a substantial length of cable to a major junction in the network. A further factor is that the developer may be charged the cost of lost telephone call revenue if it is necessary to disconnect lines during the development of the site.

Trees

Although some sites for example in town or city centres may be completely devoid of natural vegetation many sites do contain trees and hedgerows. This even includes sites within towns where houses are to be redeveloped at a higher density or an old factory estate is redeveloped. The planning authority will certainly consider the desirability of retaining such trees and the developer must be aware of this when assessing the feasibility of a new development. On greenfield sites trees and hedgerows may be evident and quite apart from the wishes of the planning authority they can be regarded as a bonus feature in any development proposal, provided that they are not right in the way of a proposed access or building!

In evaluating the significance of trees on a site it is important to find out whether they are protected by a Tree Preservation Order. This is an Order made by the local authority under the Town and Country Planning Act 1990. The effect of it is to protect the trees from being cut down or lopped without the consent of the planning authority. To contravene an Order can result in a fine and/or imprisonment.

Local authorities often make such Orders in an opportunistic way, that is to say in response to a possible threat to their future. This is in no sense a criticism of the approach because authorities have plenty of other things to be doing besides making Tree Preservation Orders. However, it does mean that even though trees on a development site may not now be protected, the authority may place an Order on them as soon as a planning application is submitted. The developer should take careful account of this possibility when examining a site. Although the Planning Act gives the local authority fairly tough powers in respect of trees, the authority must use the power with discrimination. It should make an Order only for trees that are good specimens and worthy of protection.

Trees are important too in the design and location of new development. Where the developer proposes to retain trees on a site, any new structure will need to be a certain distance away from the trees for two reasons. First, the structure could damage the tree or its roots if it is built too close. Secondly, the tree's own roots could damage a new building if it is built too close to them. Poplars and willows are notorious for sending out roots which may damage foundations or sewers.

Detailed advice on how near buildings can safely come to trees is given in a publication of the British Standards Institution, BS5387. The presence of trees on a site constrains development not only during construction but also in the longer term, since the developer must take account of the relationship between a tree and building assuming the tree has reached its full size. A simple rule of thumb during the construction stage is that no construction activity should come within the spread of a tree or a distance equivalent to half the height of the tree, whichever is the greater. For the longer term the distance which buildings should be from the centre of a tree will vary according to the species of tree, but generally this is less of a constraint on development than the constraint posed during construction work.

The constraint of trees may well determine the amount of development that can take place on a site. Whilst the principle of the development may not be at stake the amount is, and therefore the sum of money that someone is prepared to pay for the site.

Site Boundaries

Conveyance plans often raise questions about boundaries because they are drawn at too small a scale, or the line on the conveyance plan is roughly drawn. Although the area enclosed by a boundary may be clear cut, the detail of the boundary itself can be confusing. This is a matter of concern for several reasons. First of all, who is responsible for the boundary? Many disputes arise over this question. It may make a big difference whether a substantial brick wall round a site is the responsibility of the site owner or adjoining owners. The same question of responsibility may arise if the boundary is defined by a hedge or fence.

A fence or wall on a boundary may be the responsibility of either adjoining landowner; it depends on what is set out in the title deeds of the property. The same goes for a hedge, but where there is a ditch adjoining the hedge it is normally the case that the ownership boundary lies on the side of the ditch furthest away from the hedge. Assume there is a field 'A' with a hedge on one boundary, a ditch beyond, then there is a field 'B'. The owner of field 'A' is normally the owner of both the hedge and the ditch. Where the boundary of a property is a river or stream the ownership of the property normally extends to the middle of the river or stream.

In a built-up area the development property may have other buildings on its boundaries. This raises a number of issues. If there is a building on the development site, will its demolition affect the stability of buildings on either side? When a new building is erected on the site, can it physically abut adjoining buildings (assuming no windows on the abutting elevations)?

The general position is that there is no natural right of support for buildings (whereas there is a natural right of support for land). However, the owner of a building may acquire a right of support by specific grant or by usage; and this acquired right is in the nature of an easement. If one is contemplating a redevelopment which affects adjoining property it must be remembered that to damage the support of that property is actionable at law because it constitutes a nuisance.

In theory, there is no reason why one should not build right up against an adjoining wall; the problem is, where does the boundary of ownership between the two properties lie, since clearly one cannot build on someone else's land. At common law there are in fact rights to carry out work to a party wall, that is a wall that constitutes the boundary between two properties and in London, for example, there is detailed guidance in the London Building Act, now replaced by the Building Regulations, on what can and cannot be done to a party wall.

Boundaries are also important from a town planning point of view. What happens on the boundary may influence whether a site appears 'well-contained' to the planners, or whether it is 'exposed'. A strong hedgeline is often helpful in putting the case for a development proposal. To contain a development is, to some extent, to control it, and control is beloved of planners.

5 Legal Ownership

This section deals with aspects of site evaluation that are more important to the developer/landowner than the local authority. It is essential for the former to know what restrictions there are upon a site and to establish that he can acquire good title to the property.

It may seem out of place to include a section on ownership in the evaluation of development sites. It should be apparent who owns a site or property and if the owner is not prepared to sell then the developer will walk away. The question of ownership is arguably of less concern to the local authority, since planning is concerned primarily with the use of land and not ownership.

Despite this, there are a number of reasons why some consideration can usefully be given to ownership. First of all ownership may be more complex than one expects; it may be leasehold rather than freehold; it may be constrained by various 'charges'. This will have a bearing on the site's development potential. Secondly, planning authorities should have regard to ownership because it may have land-use implications. Thus a site which may be suitable for development from a planning point of view may not be developable because it is subject to a restriction that it be used only for say, allotments or a playing field. Since the local authority is required to ensure that there is enough land available to meet forecast needs it must be prepared to discount such sites and look elsewhere. Finally, there is some practical value in having a brief understanding of land ownership, although this aspect of the development process will normally be dealt with in detail by a solicitor.

Establishing Title

Normally, the individual or company who is seeking to acquire a site for development will know who the owner is. Thus he may read in the trade press about a site or property being available; or he may be advised of it by a local agent. Sometimes, though, the developer will not know. He may see a site on his travels which he reckons has potential but he does not know the owner. Unfortunately there is no simple or foolproof way of ascertaining ownership. The Land Registry (which is described more fully later) will not tell an enquirer who it is that owns a particular parcel of land or building. The index of registered land which they hold is private and in any event is arranged by title number rather than postal address. Thus, a member of the public cannot simply contact the Registry and ask to look at a particular entry in the register. He must have the owner's permission. Secondly, because the index gives title numbers rather than places it is impossible to ask for details of a place; one has to ask for the details held under a particular title number, which clearly presupposes that one knows the landowner and has his permission to consult the register. This situation will change with the Land Registration Act 1990. Under the Act it is now possible to go to the Registry and find out the owner of registered land. The situation with unregistered land, though, remains as before.

Since it is not possible to find out the owner from the Land Registry in the case of unregistered land there are a number of lines of enquiry to ascertain ownership but they have no guarantee of success. In the past it was possible to consult the register at the rates office of the local authority since all properties and land which had rateable value were included in their records together with the name of the ratepayer. One shortcoming of this line of inquiry was that vacant property and farmland, on which no rates are paid, did not appear on the rates records. This source of information will not vary with the new community charge system. A register of community charge payers with their addresses is kept at the local authority offices. So far as business property is concerned it is subject to a Uniform Business Rate and a register of ratepayers is maintained by the local authority.

If it is not possible to ascertain ownership from the rates office, another line of inquiry is the planning department of the local authority. If a property has a planning history the name of the owner will appear on the planning application. However, there is no certainty that the owner will still be the same as at the time of the application. If all else fails it is a question of making local enquiries in the vicinity of the site in case there is someone who knows.

The Nature of Ownership

Assuming, though, that the owner is known, it is still essential to make certain enquiries about the property. Obviously, one needs to verify the owner's claim to the property. First it is necessary to know whether title to the property is registered or unregistered, that is to say, whether it has been registered with the Land Registry under the Land Registration Act 1925. This can be done by searching the Public Index Map at the District Land Registry. Not all land is registered; although the system of registration was initiated in 1925, parts of the country, particularly in rural areas, are not yet covered. Moreover, even in areas where registration is compulsory, registration will only occur when a property changes ownership.

In the case of unregistered land the vendor of the property must produce to the purchaser an abstract of title which proves that he has a good title to the land. This can be a fairly complicated business and may involve investigation of several title deeds dating back over a period of at least 15 years (this being the necessary period required to demonstrate ownership under the Law of Property Act 1925 as amended). It is more usual nowadays for the vendor to produce an epitome of title rather than an abstract of title the former being a more simple presentation of the title information.

If the land or property is registered the owner does not need to produce an abstract of title; he need only prove to the purchaser that he is the registered proprietor of the land. This will appear on the title held at the Land Registry. The owner is given a Land Certificate which is equivalent to the title deeds of unregistered land and all he need do is produce the Certificate as proof of ownership.

The title at the District Land Registry is made up of three registers, namely the Property Register, the Proprietorship Register and the Charges Register. The Property Register briefly describes the property, includes a plan showing its extent and gives details of rights which the land enjoys over other property; the Proprietorship Register describes the class of title owned by the proprietor and his name and address; the Charges Register lists encumbrances affecting the property. It is best if a solicitor investigates the title of the vendor of a site and he will do this by checking the title documents of the vendor, and tracing them back for a period of at least 15 years. Having established a good title the solicitor will need to tie the title documents to the identity of the site, to ensure that the title is good for the whole site being considered. Sometimes a site may have been in two separate ownerships in the past so it is important to ensure that the current vendor has title over the entire site.

Another problem is the identity of the site. The site may seem obvious on the ground but it needs to be described and detailed on a plan. Normally a written description of the site, for example, No.1 High Street, Anytown; its area in square metres or whatever; and a scaled plan identifying the extent of the site will provide a good starting point. Ideally, the plan should be based on the Ordnance Survey plan of the area or, failing that, it should be based on a site survey. A sketch is not satisfactory.

Having identified the site and title to it the solicitor will wish to investigate the rights which the site enjoys. As noted above, they are listed in the Property Register. The most important right is that of access and this should also be apparent from an inspection of the site. If there is no access, the solicitor may advise the developer/owner of the site that further evaluation would be fruitless since in most cases a development site depends on a vehicular access being available.

Tenancies

The highest form of ownership is freehold and it offers the greatest flexibility to the purchaser. Nevertheless it may be subject to other interests in the property which restrict the developer. Two principal interests are leases and tenancies. It is to be noted that leases of less than 21 years, and tenancies, do not normally appear on the register of a registered title or the abstract in the case of unregistered land. Therefore, the purchasers' solicitor should enquire whether such overriding interests in the site exist.

If a property is subject to a long lease the developer will need to acquire the leasehold interest and he will first wish to know the length of lease and any restrictions in the lease which will affect his ability to develop the property.

The presence of a tenant in a property whether residential, agricultural or business may severely restrict the ability of a developer to carry out a project involving redevelopment of the property. There are statutory rules and common law which determine when a tenant can be evicted from property; it is beyond the scope of this book to examine the law in detail but a few general remarks may provide some helpful pointers.

Where the tenant is a business tenant it is possible to evict him if the tenancy has ended and the landlord (that is, the developer in this case) intends to demolish or reconstruct the premises. If the tenancy has not ended there is no right of eviction and the landlord must negotiate with the tenant or await the end of the tenancy.

Residential tenants are protected by the Rent Act 1977 or the Housing Act 1988. The circumstances in which a tenancy under either Act may be terminated are complex. Generally speaking it is easier for a landlord to obtain repossession of a property where the tenancy was created by the 1988 Act. This is particularly relevant in the case of redevelopment proposals, since the 1988 Act has introduced as a ground for repossession that he proposes to redevelop the property. This ground does not apply to 1977 Act tenancies. Thus, a property which has a 1977 Act tenant in occupation will be significantly less attractive to a developer than one occupied by a 1988 Act tenancy.

Agricultural tenancies are protected by the Agricultural Holding Act 1986. The Act generally confers security of tenure on the tenant and it specifies five grounds on which a tenancy can be terminated. For the purpose of development sites the relevant ground is the fifth, which states that a tenant may be evicted if the landlord proposes to use the land for a non-agricultural purpose, and has planning permission therefor.

Legal Restrictions

Next it is necessary to find out whether there are any charges or other restrictions on the property; this necessitates contacting the District Land Registry in the case of registered land and the Central Land Registry in other cases. The charges fall into two main categories:

a) Financial charges on the land.
b) Restrictions on the use of the land.

The Land Charges Department of the District Land Registry holds five registers of which the most important is the Land Charges Register. This lists, for the property in question, certain classes of charge upon the property. Examples would be public rights of way, covenants, leases and mortgages.

Local Restrictions

The District and Central Land Registries between them deal with non-local charges. Local charges are detailed in the Local Land Charges Register whether the land is registered or not. This register is kept by the district or borough council in the area.

There are twelve parts in the register covering the following charges:

1 General financial charges
2 Specific financial charges
3 Planning charges
4 Miscellaneous charges
5 Charges for maintenance of ways over fenlands
6 Land compensation charges
7 New town charges
8 Civil aviation charges
9 Open-cast coal mining charges
10 Listed building charges
11 Light obstruction notices
12 Drainage scheme charges.

Many of the parts of the register deal with fairly uncommon situations, for example, improvements to fenland waterways, and the council's reply will refer only to those parts of the register where there is any information. Usually the most relevant parts will be those dealing with planning matters. To find out what these charges are the solicitor contacts the local authority and requisitions a search, using a standard form for the purpose. The local authority completes the part of the form relating to the result of the search. Normally it takes the form of a Schedule which lists the various charges on the property. For example, Part 3 of the Schedule lists planning charges; Part 10 details listed building charges.

The solicitor will also find out details of other restrictions which cannot be entered as charges, by contacting the district council. The solicitor does not need to know the name of the owner of the property in question but simply has to include an Ordnance Survey plan with his request for information.

These 'enquiries' as they are called are made on a standard form which consists of two parts: Part I comprises 18 questions and Part II has 13. They cover the following matters:

Part 1

1 Is the highway adopted?
2 Is there a road improvement scheme?
3 Notice issued under Public Health/Housing/Highways Act?
Contravention of Building Regulations?
5 Public sewers available?
6 Enforcement Notice served?
7 Status of structure and local plans for the area?
8 Article 4 direction (restricting permitted development)?
9 Revocation/Discontinuance Order or TPO?
10 Existing use compensation paid?
11 Details of planning decisions?
12 In a Conservation Area?
13 Building Preservation Notice served?
14 Compulsory Purchase Order?
15 In a slum clearance area or General Improvement Area?
16 In a smoke control area?
17 Unoccupied, but liable to rates?
18 In an area of compulsory land registration?

Part II

1 Public path across site?
2 Road or path being stopped up or diverted?
3 Application to display advertisement or in area of advertisement control?
4 Listed Building?
5 Repairs Notice served?
6 Completion Notice served?
7 In a National Park or Area of Outstanding Natural Beauty?
8 Underground pipeline?
9 In multiple occupation?
10 In noise abatement zone?
11 In an area of an Urban Development Corporation?
12 In an Enterprise Zone?
13 In an Industrial Improvement Area?

As if the above enquiries were not enough, the purchaser may on occasions also need to check whether the property is registered as a common or town or village green. It will normally be apparent when such enquiries are unnecessary; if it appears that the property might be so registered the solicitor will contact the county council who maintain a register of common land. If a site is wholly or partly common land the developer would be well advised to steer clear of it because it is extremely difficult to obtain the necessary legal consent to acquire such land as is needed for the development.

It will become evident that such charges can have an important bearing on the evaluation of a site. The financial charges may not be crucial in the decision whether to develop or not, but they could affect the price that is paid for the property.

Easements

A site or building may be subject to an easement which could have a bearing on its development potential. A right of way or right of light are both examples of easements.

The right of light to an adjoining building may mean that the site being considered can only be developed to a certain height or over a certain area. The owner of the site may know whether there is such an easement over his property because it may be referred to in the deed of conveyance of the property. On the other hand the adjoining owner may acquire such an easement if he has enjoyed the right of light for the previous 20 years.

Is there anything the landowner can do to get rid of such an easement? In practice the owner can only get rid of it with the agreement of the other party which is a matter of private negotiation.

The other main easement that can affect the development potential of a site is a right of way which can be acquired or removed in broadly the same way as a right of light. Often it will be possible to tell by looking at a site whether an adjoining owner has an easement over it, for example, because there is a house or footpath close by, or pipes cross the site.

Restrictive Covenants

Restrictive covenants are similar in some respect to easements and, like them, they can affect the development potential of a site. They are rights enjoyed by the owners of adjoining land but they may be more far-reaching than easements. Like easements they will normally be apparent from the deed of conveyance of the property. They cannot be removed except by recourse to the Lands Tribunal.

It is possible for a covenant to be removed by the Lands Tribunal if the person seeking to discharge the covenant can show that the reason for the imposition of the covenant is no longer valid. It will require a clear indication of a change of circumstances to prove that the covenant is out of date. It is unlikely a covenant recently made could be discharged.

S106 Agreements are another form of legal restriction. Section 106 of the Town and Country Planning Act 1990 enables anyone to enter into an agreement with the local planning authority which regulates the use or development of land. Normally it will be the owner or prospective purchaser of land who enters into such an Agreement and typically it will require the owner to contribute some infrastructure works, public open space, village hall or similar if he carries out a specified development. The reasoning behind this requirement is that sometimes a development may not be acceptable unless the developer undertakes to carry out certain works. A new housing estate, for example, might need a narrow stretch of road to be widened because of the extra traffic it will cause. Requirements such as this can sometimes be covered by a condition on a planning permission but that is not always very satisfactory from the local authority's point of view. Therefore, Section 106 of the Act allows for developers to 'enter into' an Agreement, which is stronger than a planning condition, and which secures the necessary local improvements to make the proposed development acceptable. We say 'enter into' in quotation marks because in reality the developer is often advised that he will not get planning permission unless he does meet the local authority's requirements. Just what the authority can ask for when a developer applies for permission is a matter of considerable controversy which goes beyond the scope of this book. A S106 Agreement runs with the land and anyone who subsequently buys the land with the intention of carrying out the scheme to which the Agreement relates should be aware that he too will be subject to the Agreement. Accordingly, it is essential for the developer when evaluating a site to be fully aware of the Agreement which could represent a significant burden on its development cost.

A S106 Agreement can be revoked if the developer can demonstrate that it is no longer relevant. The local authority may itself agree to the revocation of the Agreement but, if it refuses to, then the landowner has to apply to the Lands Tribunal.

Whether the Lands Tribunal will allow the restriction to be lifted depends very much on whether, in planning terms, the restriction has become obsolete. For example, in 1989 applicants sought to remove a

restriction on a house in Henley-on-Thames which prevented the house being used for office purposes. Planning permission was granted for change of use to offices in 1986 and the applicants wanted to lift the restriction in order to implement the planning permission. The Lands Tribunal dismissed the application. They considered that the restriction was still relevant because there was no evidence that someone would not want to live in the house. The fact that planning permission had been given for the change of use to offices did not invalidate the reasons for the imposition of the S106 Agreement (for details of this case see Journal of Planning Law 1989 pages 622 and 623).

Access is a particularly important ingredient of a development site and the next parts of this chapter deal with various aspects of access and the problems that may be encountered.

Rights of Way

These may be public or private and they may confer various rights of passage across property. Public rights of way can be fairly easily discovered from the county council. Obviously, a road is likely to involve a public right of way, but not necessarily. There are still many private roads around the country. One check on the status of a road is to find out from the county council if they have adopted it as a public right of way under the Highways Act 1959. If they have adopted it then the road is public. If they have not adopted it the road may be public or it may be private. The county council can usually advise. This has serious implications for the developer. He may acquire a development site only to discover that the road leading to it is not public. He then has to find out who owns it or has rights of way across it. In practice this can mean negotiating with numerous householders on either side of the road. The developer also needs to consider the future maintenance of the road. If it is private the responsibility for maintenance lies with the households on either side unless it is known to be in one individual's ownership. Some of the responsibility, and therefore cost, could fall on the owner of the development site and he would wish to take this into account when assessing its value. In the long term it is often preferable for the road to be adopted by the highway authority who take on the responsibility for future maintenance. However, they will do so only when the road is made up to an adoptable standard which could involve substantial cost.

Roads are more properly called highways which by definition are roads over which the public have a right of way. As well as roads there are roads used as public paths (RUPPs for short), bridleways, footpaths. All such ways confer a right of passage by the public across land. Where a right of way crosses a site can the developer do anything about it? The answer is yes. He may apply to stop it up or divert it. There are set procedures either under the Highways Act 1980, or the Town and Country Planning Act 1990. These procedures require a developer to apply for permission from the Departments of the Environment and Transport. He can do so only when planning permission has been obtained; therefore he should discuss this point with the planning and highway authorities when he submits the planning application.

As to which act he relies upon, it is normal to use the Planning Act when the diversion is required for planning reasons as part of a development proposal; and the Highways Act if the diversion is required for highways reasons.

In minor cases the developer may be able to apply direct to a magistrates court but this too will involve a hearing if there are any objections which cannot be resolved beforehand.

As a general point it may be said that diversion of a footpath is a less controversial step than stopping it up. If the footpath is well used there could be considerable opposition to its closure; it may be more prudent to offer an alternative route which is still convenient for people on foot.

Ransom Strips

A not infrequent occurrence is where a small but essential part of a development site proves not to belong to the owner selling the site. Where a third party owns property which is needed to enable development to occur that party may exercise a ransom over that site. The question is: What is that ransom worth? This question was addressed in the case of Stokes v Cambridge.

The case is widely quoted in negotiations over the acquisition of access and it is therefore worth describing it briefly. The Cambridge City Council wished to acquire land from Mr. Stokes for the purpose of industrial development. The Council already owned the means of access to Stokes' land. In deciding how much compensation Stokes was due the Land Tribunal concluded that the City Council's control of the access was worth one-third of the development value of Stokes' land, and awarded accordingly.

Thus, where the access to a development site is controlled by a public authority the Stokes v Cambridge case suggests that up to one third of the value of the site may need to be foregone to the ransom holder. However, if the owner of the access is not a public authority and the person wishing to acquire, is also not vested with statutory powers to acquire, then it is entirely a matter of negotiation as to what proportion of the development value must be forgone. Although Stokes v Cambridge is often quoted at the outset in private negotiations it is very important to remember that the ransom holder can ask for whatever percentage of development value, or whatever price, he or she likes.

6 Marketing

The assessment of whether a development proposal is marketable is critical to the evaluation process. In the first place it will influence whether a site is even considered to be a development site or not — if there is no market for a superstore in a small town, no site within the town can be regarded as a development site for this purpose. Secondly, it has an obvious bearing on the value of the site. Assume two pieces of land on the edge of a town, one of 0.4 ha (1 acre) and the other of 20 ha (50 acres). Both are proposed for housing, but the larger site would take ten years to develop. If the value of the smaller site is £500 000, that of the larger site will have a lower value on a pro rata basis because the site will take much longer to develop and market. Half the larger site may not be developed for say five years. This half will be less valuable than the area that can be developed and sold immediately. If someone pays £500 000 for 0.4 ha (an acre) of land which generates a return in one year he will pay less, now, for 0.4 ha (an acre) of land that generates the same return, but in three year's time. The reason is that the return in one year's time could then be invested so that in three year's time it would produce, say, an extra 40 per cent, compared with the land that does not produce a return until the five years have elapsed.

In looking, then, at the market potential of a site, one has to decide not only if a site is marketable, but also how long it may take to market and therefore how much one should pay for it.

In this section we shall look at some of the factors that are relevant to marketing and how one might weigh them up in a methodical way.

Marketing considerations are of varying importance according to the type of development that the developer is proposing. It is generally true that no developer, whether he is a housebuilder or retail park specialist, will carry out a development for which there is no market; nevertheless, the housebuilder has a known market, usually comprising thousands of potential homeowners in a given area,

79

whereas the retail park specialist is dependent on a small number of retailers who may be seeking location in a particular town. Thus to continue the example, the retail park developer is to a far greater degree market-led. The nature of retail park development, and indeed much commercial development, is also more 'lumpy' than residential development where the units of construction are more readily divisible. Table 6.1 illustrates what is meant by 'lumpy'. The housing estate begins to produce a return in year 2 and this continues smoothly throughout years 3 to 5. By contrast, the commercial development, in this case an office block, is constructed over two years, involving a very substantial outlay. The block is sold in year 3, producing a single, large receipt.

Table 6.1   Cash flow

	Year 1 £	Year 2 £	Year 3 £	Year 4 £	Year 5 £
Housing costs	200 000	200 000	200 000	200 000	200 000
estate returns	–	250 000	250 000	250 000	250 000
Office costs	600 000	600 000	–	–	–
block returns	–		– 2 000 000	–	–

The second point is that marketing is of greater concern to the developer than to the local planning authority. The former actually has to sell a building. It follows that a piece of land may be a development site in the eyes of a planning authority, but not in those of the developer. An important exception is in the case of housing where the Department of the Environment have advised local authorities that there should be sufficient land to meet housing needs in areas where people want to live.

Paragraph 11 of Department of the Environment Circular 15/84 states:

It is essential that sufficient land is genuinely available in practical terms to enable the policies and proposals in approved structure plans and adopted local plans to be carried forward. This means that sites must not only be free, or easily freed, from planning, physical and ownership constraints but also be capable of being developed economically, be in areas where potential house buyers want to live, and be suitable for the wide range of housing types which the housing market now requires.

One can think of many examples where authorities propose sites for housing development which the market is less than enthusiastic about.

There is almost a probability in certain areas that the authority's choice of housing sites will differ from that of the housebuilding industry because planners will tend to choose sites whose development would not unduly harm the character of an adjoining area and perhaps cause least local opposition. It is easier to allocate a single 20-ha (50-acre) site for housing on the edge of a medium-sized town where it adjoins suburbia than ten 2-ha (5-acres) sites on the edges of villages which have Conservation Areas. This approach is well exemplified in Oxfordshire, where the County Strategy is to direct most housing development to four county towns rather than villages or new settlements. There has been some resistance to housebuilding in Didcot with very slow rates of development in the town, albeit in the late 1980s the situation was changing through the lack of alternative sites in the surrounding area.

What is the Competition?

This question is relevant whether one is considering a new housing estate, an office block, a shopping arcade or a greengrocer's shop. The subject matter of the investigation will vary from one type of development to another, but similar criteria apply. Let us suppose that the development site under consideration is for a possible industrial scheme. It extends to some 2 ha (5 acres) and ABC Developments Ltd are considering its acquisition. They propose to erect B1 units on the site. Their investigation will need to cover how much B1 space is currently on the market in the surrounding area, or has planning permission but is not yet started or is allocated in a local plan for the area. Secondly, it will be necessary to find out the rate at which B1 space has been taken up over the last few years, for example 14 000 m^2 (150 000 square feet) per year. Thirdly, the developer will wish to appraise the quality of the competition. So far as evaluating the site is concerned, the main criteria will include location to the main road network, proximity to labour supply and character of the surrounding area. Thus whilst there may be a considerable supply of industrial land in a given area the site being examined may still prove highly marketable if it has clear locational or other advantages over the competition.

Local agents may be able to advise the developer on the above points although there are two limitations to be borne in mind; first, an agent's knowledge is likely to be most complete in respect of the developments which his practice is involved in; secondly, agents may not have the time or inclination to provide too much detailed information unless they are instructed to handle the acquisition of the site or its subsequent disposal. At least one practice has started making charges for the supply of information.

An alternative source of information is the local authority whose planning or commercial departments may be able to help. In Berkshire for example the County Council maintains a register of industrial commitments which is updated annually. However, this register has shortcomings in that it does not show the rate of uptake of industrial buildings. The register shows the location of the site, its size and when planning permission was given for industrial development of the site. Another shortcoming of the local authority as a source of advice is that it is unlikely to be able or willing to give a view on the relative attractiveness of competing sites. It is not the job of local authorities to offer this service and the developer will have to rely upon his judgement or that of a commercial agent.

Location

In property development it has been said that the three most important characteristics of a site are location, location and location. In the following pages a brief comment is made on various types of development, highlighting their particular locational requirements. Proximity to a main road is seen as the most important feature for several types of development, for example, hotels, business parks, superstores and filling stations, but it is not true of others such as housing or shops. The purpose of the following comments is to help in answering the question: Would this site be a good site for a hotel (or factory or whatever)?

Hotels

Hotel sites must meet certain well-defined criteria if they are to be acceptable to the hotelier from a marketing point of view. These criteria stem from the simple fact that most hotels rely on the business traveller for their principal custom. Therefore, hotels should be easily accessible to the main road network, which means that they should not only be visible from a main road but also easy to reach. It is no good for a hotel to be visible from a motorway if to reach the hotel involves an awkward drive through side roads and housing estates. Since the main customer for hotels is normally the businessman the suitability of a site for a hotel will depend on its proximity to employment and business areas. A seaside town with little employment will not attract new hotel development even on sites close to the main road into the town. On the other hand, a town or city with a substantial commercial or industrial base will be generally attractive to hoteliers.

Within this context a site needs to be of adequate size. This varies according to the type of hotel being proposed. A small lodge-type hotel, which may be related to a roadside service station or restaurant, may require less than 0.4 ha (1 acre) of land; a 3–4 star hotel would normally need at least 100 bedrooms to run efficiently and, allowing for at least one parking space per bedroom plus manoeuvring areas and landscaping, the resulting size is about 1.6 ha (4 acres) minimum.

Adjoining land uses also play a part. A medium to upper range hotel requires a prestigious setting. This need not rule out a site on an industrial estate — for example, the new hotel at Tachbrook Park in Leamington adjoins modern B1 developments, and in Swindon Ibis have developed a hotel within the Delta Business Park on the west side of the town. However, it is unlikely that a hotel would locate on old industrial estates or in areas of cheap housing.

Perhaps the ideal site for a hotel from a hotelier's point of view is alongside a motorway or trunk road junction, or one of the principal approaches to a large town. Such a location offers visibility, accessibility, room for parking and quite probably less competition from alternative land uses which have traditionally outbid hotel development.

Housing

Housing sites are probably the most flexible of all types of development so far as their size is concerned. At one extreme a plot that can accommodate only a single dwelling may represent a viable site; going up the scale, sites of 2–4 ha (5–10) acres are an ideal size for a large number of housebuilders because they are sufficiently large for a housebuilding company to carry out a development economically; on the other hand they are not so large that the housebuilder is confronted with a massive capital outlay on day one through purchase of the site. Where the landowner owns a substantial area, for example, in excess of 20 ha (50 acres), a housebuilder may well wish to join with others as a consortium in purchasing the land, or enter into an agreement with other housebuilders to off-load some of the land at an early date in order to achieve a satisfactory cashflow. A further possibility is staged purchase, whereby the housebuilder acquires the land in phases and this may be advantageous to the vendor from a tax point of view.

It follows from the above that sites for housebuilding come in a variety of sizes and, when evaluating a particular site, one need not be too constrained by this factor.

Housing sites also come in a variety of shapes. By the nature of housing development, it is possible to bend access roads this way and that, to arrange houses in a variety of ways and to plan the number of individual units of housing according to the size of site.

The location of housing development is perhaps more sensitive. Private housing development is very responsive to its immediate surroundings. When a plot of land is offered to a housebuilder he will at the outset examine the adjoining land uses. Some uses, for example an industrial estate, may deter him altogether from pursuing the acquisition of the site. More frequently, the adjoining uses will not deter the housebuilder entirely but will dictate the type of housing which he considers marketable and may therefore affect the price he is prepared to pay. To give an example, Plan 12 shows a site on the edge of Westbury in Wiltshire which is proposed for housing development. The northern part of the site adjoins an area of local authority housing, the central part of the site adjoins inter-war and post-war semi-detached housing, while the southern part of the site is next to the village High Street of Westbury Leigh which has a variety of properties, some of which are in spacious gardens or are several hundred years old. The development of this site envisages high density housing at the northern end (about 35 dwellings per hectare), low density at the

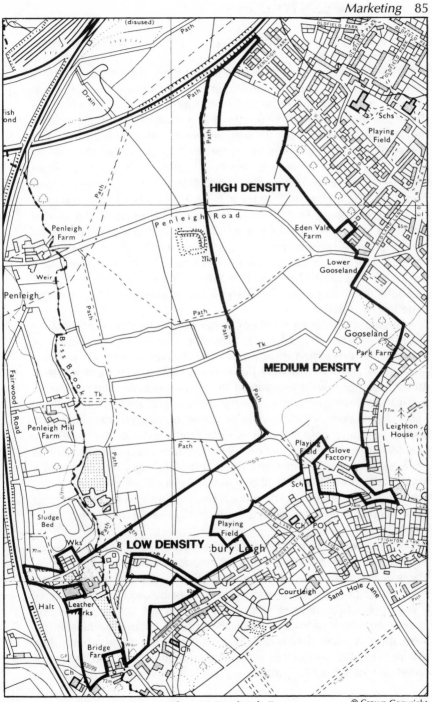

Plan 12 Penleigh Farm

southern end (20 dwellings per hectare) and medium (28 dwellings per hectare) in the middle.

Access to housing sites is less important than to sites such as those for hotels or retail stores. People are prepared to drive along side roads to reach a housing site in an attractive setting. On the other hand, if they have to go through a run-down or unattractive area to reach a housing site, this will prove a strong deterrent to its marketing.

Having established the physical factors that determine the type of housing appropriate to the site, the housebuilder must also investigate the market for different types of housing in the area. Is the demand from first time buyers looking for a 1- or 2-bedroomed terrace house? Or is there a shortage of detached housing in the area? The market appraisal may reveal a strong demand in two or three segments of the market and the housebuilder will endeavour to fit that demand to the site characteristics. It must also be remembered that on a large site (4 ha (10 acres) or more) the housebuilder will normally wish to have a variety of house types, because it results in a more attractive scheme which benefits house sales.

Applying these points to the example of Westbury, the market may at the time be for starter homes. With this in mind the developer will increase the proportion of houses in this market segment as far as is reasonable and will probably develop the northern part of the site at an early rather than later stage. If the market was for large detached houses the developer might alter the phasing and start at the southern end. The market can change in a matter of months and what may appear a highly desirable site at one time may become unsellable later. Evaluation, and valuation, of a site must have regard to such changes, particularly where the site is relatively small. This is because a small site may have little if any scope for a variety of house types; secondly, its character will be more heavily influenced by the character of the surrounding area. A larger site may be able to create its own character.

Other factors which the housebuilder will take account of when evaluating a site are the presence of various amenities in the area. These are often reflected in the sales particulars when the houses have been built, for example, proximity to train or bus service; presence of shops, golf clubs, school (especially if it has a good reputation), church, park and so on, or simply the general outlook of the site. An evaluation of a site should list any such amenities, together with their distance from the site. It is difficult to quantify the effect that such amenities have on the value of a site; at the end of the day the housebuilder will have to make a best guess, perhaps relying on the value of a comparable site if by chance there should be one.

Roadside Services

Under this heading we may include petrol filling stations, cafés and motels. There is an obvious and clear relationship between a petrol filling station and a public road; the same applies to the roadside cafes and motels operated by large companies, which sprang up throughout the UK in the period 1975–90.

The space requirements of a filling station may be quite modest and even a 0.2 ha (0.5 acre) site would be sufficient to provide a basic facility comprising eight pumps and kiosk. The essential features are first of all that the site adjoins a road which carries substantial traffic flows, for example 13 000 vehicles per 18 hours (two-way flow) could be regarded as a minimum. To put this into perspective, a dual carriageway in a provincial location might carry around 20 000–25 000 vehicles in both directions over an 18-hour day. The choice of an 18-hour day simply reflects the fact that throughout the 24 hours of a day the vast majority of traffic uses a road between the hours of 6 a.m. and 12 p.m. The traffic flow data is converted by oil companies into a forecast of petrol sales based on experience elsewhere, and it is this forecast which will determine whether a site is considered to be suitable for development and also what price will be paid for it.

Information on traffic flows on a given road is often available from the highway department of a local authority. In a town where there has been significant change, for example, with new housing, it is important to check the date of the traffic flow survey since the results may be much lower than is now the case. Very often, though, a site finder will actually rely on his own impressions from visiting the site and observing traffic over a relatively short period of time, to decide whether there is enough passing traffic to justify a new station. He will of course take into account other filling stations in the area, especially if they are on the same side of the road as the site being considered.

Motorists do not like to make a right turn across traffic to enter a station. The vast majority of a station's turnover will come from traffic on the same side of the road as the station. It is worth stating too that if the site adjoins a dual carriageway, traffic on only one carriageway will be the relevant volume of traffic to take into account.

Secondly, access and visibility must be good. This means that a site should not only have sufficient frontage width such that a way in and way out can be provided, it must also be visible from a distance, so that the motorist can safely and conveniently slow down and enter the station. It is no good if the station is tucked round a bend in the road where a motorist only sees it when he is almost on top of it.

The amount of traffic on a road, and therefore the suitability of a site for a station, depends on both the status of a road and its usage. Thus service stations are to be found on busy roads within and on the edges of towns, on main roads between towns and as part of major car-borne shopping developments.

From a town planning point of view it is worth remembering that there is clear advice from the Department of the Environment on the need for filling stations. Planning Policy Guidance Note No. 13 states that:

> It will normally be reasonable to expect a driver to travel at least 12 miles along a primary route before finding a petrol filling station and related facilities. However, 25 miles would normally represent the maximum interval which is acceptable between petrol filling stations on the same side of a primary route.

It is quite possible that a developer may judge a site to be very marketable for a filling station, whereas it does not meet the need criteria set out in the PPG. The fact that it does not meet the criteria does not mean that permission for the filling station will be refused. Rather it means that the developer will not be able to present such a strong case for the development of the site.

Shops

Shop location cannot be reduced to a simple rule. There are several factors at work, and one or more of these may have a bearing on one's assessment of a development site.

One factor is the proximity of the development site to anchor traders. If the site is close to a major multiple store it is likely to have relatively high shopper flows passing by. As a retail development it would be attractive to another multiple trader or one that can afford the high rents that are likely to be sought. In such a location one has to consider whether the site is of a size and shape that would appeal to such a trader.

If the site is remote from the main shopping magnets and is in a secondary location it is important to consider whether there is a demand for secondary shopping and the likely rental that could be achieved. This will determine the value of the development and what should be paid for the site.

Shopping location depends on factors other than proximity to magnet traders. A site may be secondary but in an area which has a reputation for a particular type of shop, for example antique shops in Fulham Road, London, or an area of estate agents.

Again, different factors operate in the case of out-of-town or edge-of-town shopping. A site that is miles from an existing shopping centre will be successful if it is readily accessible to the shopping public and there is a shortage of the type of retail space that could be provided. Detailed studies of spending power on particular goods such as furniture, DIY products and so on are undertaken by large retail companies when assessing a development site. The spending power is compared with the known supply of retail space for the particular goods and this helps the retailer to assess the need for the particular type of shop. In the case of large stores, developers as well as the retailer will assess the market in this way since his scheme depends on accurately assessing the needs of relatively few operators.

The size of site is important. It will dictate to the prospective purchaser how many shops of a given size he can fit onto the site. A site with a 7–10 m (20–30 feet) frontage may only be able to accommodate one shop unit whereas a site with a frontage of 70 m (200 feet) could provide for several. The evaluation of the latter site must therefore consider whether the market is for small units of 100 m^2 (1 076 sq.ft) each or a single large unit of 1000 m^2 (10 760 sq.ft) or something in between. In the case of large non-food stores a single store of about 4 000 m^2 (4 3040 sq.ft) will need at least 1.2 ha (3 acres) of land to enable sufficient car parking and manoeuvring areas together with boundary landscaping. Where several stores operate together in a retail park the site will need to be 8–10 ha (20–25 acres) or more.

A further indication of the quality of a retail site is the amount of pedestrian flow that passes the site over a given period. Measurement of the flow is a relatively straightforward process and has the advantage that it can be compared with other streets in a town, or indeed other towns, in order to put the site into perspective. The results should however, pay regard to the type of customer likely to pass along the street. A flow of 10 000 persons in London's Bond Street gives a very different retail potential from a similar number of pedestrians in a provincial town.

So far as retail development sites are concerned, the effect of other development proposals can be profound and it is therefore extremely important to ascertain what other proposals there are in an area. To give an example, the Merry Hill Centre at Dudley, comprising an initial phase of 167 300 m^2 (1.8 m sq. ft) of retail space has probably affected the rate of development of new shopping schemes in Birmingham city centre. While it is unlikely to have caused the closure of shops in the city centre, it has probably accelerated the change in the types of shops there, towards high value comparison shops and away from traditional convenience shopping.

Other factors to be borne in mind are whether the road in which the development site is situated is likely to be pedestrianised or not. Pedestrianisation has traditionally been resisted by retailers for fear of losing trade and possible servicing facilities. In practice it has usually benefitted local traders because it creates a more pleasant shopping environment.

Even the side of a street can be important. One side of the same street may be popular while the other side is run down. This would normally arise if the popular side adjoins the main shopping area while the unpopular side is severed by a busy traffic route. The best way of evaluating a shopping site is often a careful walk round the shopping centre to see where pedestrian and traffic flows are most pronounced. Fleet Street in Swindon is a good example. This is a busy one-way street which forms part of the town's inner distribution route. The south side adjoins the main shopping area which is largely pedestrianised. The north side adjoins offices and car parks and is separated from the main shopping area by fairly continuous traffic. The only type of shop that can survive in such a location is a specialist shop which people will make an effort to visit.

There is a noticeable contrast too in Leeds near the railway station. The north side of the road contains the Bond Street Centre which in turn links to other main areas of city centre shopping. The south side of the road (which is heavily trafficked) comprises many run-down properties with secondary trading characteristics.

Offices

Office developments of any size are likely to be sold for investment purposes to an institution such as a pension fund or insurance company. It follows that the development will need to be acceptable to the institution and their criteria of acceptability require careful consideration. There are three main criteria: flexibility, location and car parking. Under the first heading the institutional investor will consider whether, if the building was vacated, it would be readily lettable to another tenant. Is it to a good standard or is it capable of being changed to suit a new tenant? Secondly, the building should be in an area which is acceptable to occupiers rather than being out on a limb.

It is the second broad criterion which is the main concern of site evaluation and an example from Swindon will illustrate the point. Plan 13 shows the town centre and its immediate environs. Site A was developed in the late 1960s–early 1970s; site B in the early 1980s; both sites remained vacant for a considerable period. Site C, adjoining site A enjoyed the benefit of a planning permission for over 20 years before being finally built in 1990. By contrast no less than nine office schemes have been developed in the area round the railway station which is accepted as the principal area for large offices.

The problem with site B was its location, away from any recognised office area. The site has private housing on two sides, a public house on the third side and a road frontage on the fourth side. Site A adjoined the town centre and was close to the main shopping area; however, it did not have satisfactory car parking. Although there is a public car park nearby, it is used by shoppers and is not convenient for those working in the office building. Site C is well located, albeit there is little car parking and it involves a mixed use scheme.

It does not follow that being in the right location will guarantee immediate letting of an office building. The design must be right for the market and there must be an active market. However, it is a very important factor and a well-located site will always have the edge over a secondary one.

The third factor is car parking. This is not directly relevant to site evaluation and the main point is that office development should provide ample parking, for example, one space per 70 m^2 (750 sq.ft.)

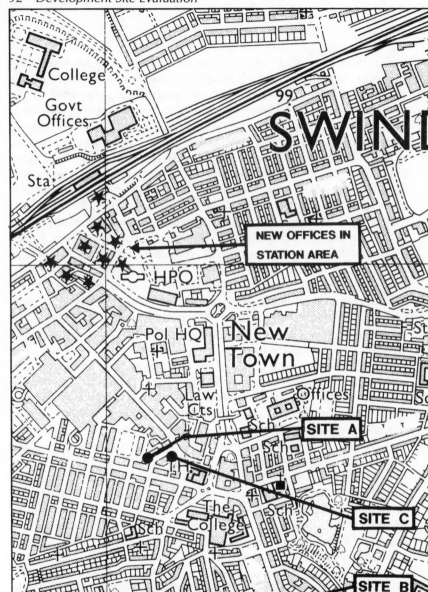

Plan 13 Swindon town centre

© Crown Copyright

of office space. The aspects of parking which do concern site evaluation are the extent of car parking nearby and whether that parking is suitable for office users. If there is a good supply of car parking in the area it may well make a site suitable for office development that one would have regarded as unsuitable because it could not provide much car parking on site.

The attitude of the planning authority towards car parking can be critical to the suitability of a site for office development. If the authority's policy is strictly to limit the provision of parking on site (for traffic control reasons) a developer may be very cautious about proceeding with a project. This is because adequate on-site parking is extremely convenient to the occupier and makes a scheme considerably more marketable. The deterrent effect of limited on-site parking will only be lessened if it is universally applied in an area so that no one building has an 'unfair advantage' over another. It will also be more acceptable to occupiers if adequate alternatives, for example multi-storey parking, park and ride schemes, are available.

Industry

Sites and buildings for industry need to be conveniently placed *vis-à-vis* the main road network. This is not because they need to be visible or accessible in the way that a hotel needs to; it is so that large lorries bringing goods from the building can do so with ease and without causing problems to local communities. By the same token an industrial site next to an area of housing may be unsuitable because of the problems of noise, pollution, etc.

Another factor to consider when appraising a site for industry is the availability of labour. This means not only that there is a ready pool of labour but also that there are good public transport links so that people can get to the industrial site easily.

7 Economic Viability

The developer should by now have established whether he is likely to get planning permission for his development and whether there are any factors that may hinder his ability to carry it out. There is also the question of whether the developer will secure an adequate financial return and it is this question which will be considered in the following pages. It is no good identifying a site which in town planning terms is fine for a particular scheme if it fails the test of economic viability. This happened in the docklands area of London in the 1970s when local authorities produced a Master Plan for redevelopment of the area, showing the development potential for each and every parcel of land. They then sat back and nothing happened—one of the reasons being that the cost of making the sites developable rendered the resulting schemes uneconomic. The London Docklands Development Corporation has subsequently invested substantially in the area through the provision of infrastructure in order to balance the economic equation. It has also adopted a very market-responsive approach to the development of the area rather than seeking to imprint its own master plan on the area.

An imaginary example may help to explain the concept of viability more precisely. Let us imagine a high street in a town where there are two adjoining shops for sale. Each shop has a floor area of 93 m² (1000 sq. ft.) on the ground floor with storage and ancillary space of 74 m² (800 sq. ft.) on the first floor. Each shop is let at £100 000 per annum.

A developer considers purchasing one of the units with a view to redevelopment. The asking price of the unit is equivalent to 15 years' rent i.e. £1 500 000. By redeveloping, the developer can increase the floorspace of the unit to 232 m² (2 500 sq. ft.) and achieve a rental income of £125 000. The capital value of the shop is estimated at £1 875 000. In order to carry out the development, the developer must spend £400 000 on building works and interest charges. The calculations are set out below.

Acquisition cost	£1 500 000
Building and interest charges	£ 400 000
Total costs	£1 900 000
Completed development value	£1 875 000

Clearly, the redevelopment of one unit would not be viable.

Another developer is aware of a demand by a retailer to establish a presence in the particular town. By redeveloping the two shops and creating one new shop on two floors the developer estimates that he can achieve a rental of £300 000 per annum. The cost of building a new shop is £400 000, comprising construction costs and interest charges. The complete calculation is set out below:

Acquisition cost	£3 000 000
Building and interest charges	£ 400 000
Total costs	£3 400 000
Completed development value	£4 000 000

In these circumstances the developer can earn a profit of £600 000, or 18 per cent of his outlay, and therefore the two shop units do constitute a significant development site in his terms.

The significance of this example is that it shows whether a site may be a development site or not. If the shops are more valuable or as valuable in their existing form as they would be if redeveloped then no developer is likely to redevelop them. There are many towns whose shopping centres include some quite elderly shops that appear ripe for development and it may puzzle the outsider why those shops still remain. The answer most probably lies in the fact that the building shells of the shops may be old but they make maximum use of the site and the selling area has been refurbished. In short, to rebuild would not create additional value.

The principle of viability can be simply stated, namely, will the development project being considered make an adequate profit such that the developer is persuaded to undertake it rather than investing his money and skills in an alternative project? Stated in this way the touchstone of viability is a minimum figure below which alternative projects are more profitable. Of course, the development in question may far exceed the minimum figure. To answer the viability question the developer will undertake a viability appraisal. This comprises an estimate of the various costs and returns of a development. The principal costs are construction costs, interest charges, acquisition fees, professional fees and land costs. The return is expressed either as rental income or a capital value.

It is possible to obtain a relatively accurate idea of construction costs and professional and acquisition fees. Construction costs data is usually provided by an architect or quantity surveyor. On large commercial schemes a reliable cost estimate is essential even before planning permission is obtained because it will help inform the developer what he can afford to pay for a site. Reference to generalised construction cost data gives a crude estimate which may be fine for a greenfield site free of any construction constraints. In reality, most sites will suffer one or more problems, which render generalised data unhelpful. Thus, in a large city, construction costs will be increased by:

a) restrictions on when contractor's vehicles may visit the site;
b) the type of crane that can operate on a restricted site;
c) the need to provide support to adjoining buildings;
d) more complicated accommodation for construction workers on site due to lack of space, for example, erection of staff cabins at high level over the pavement.

It is therefore necessary on any major redevelopment site to assess construction costs in some detail when first evaluating the site. Interest rates vary but one must make an estimate, bearing in mind that most developers (large insurance companies and offshore companies are an exception) have no control over how they may change. Current rental income can be forecast with some certainty, but one can only make an educated guess at whether rental levels will rise or fall at the first rent review. Finally, there are land costs. These are often treated as a 'residual' variable in viability appraisals, that is, they are arrived at after one has calculated all the other variables. This need not be the case. Thus the land cost may be fixed and the developer will take this datum to estimate what rental income he must achieve to make a profitable development.

The following examples will start with the normal situation where land is treated as the residual variable. Field B on the edge of town X is for sale. There is planning permission for housing at a density not exceeding 30 dwellings/ha (12 dwellings per acre). The prospective housebuilder assesses the likely selling price of the houses based on other houses in the area of a similar size, density and quality to those which he thinks most suited to the site. In this way the housebuilder estimates the end value of the development. From this value he must deduct construction costs, the housebuilder's profit, interest on the land acquisition and construction costs and sales costs. Having deducted the costs of the development from its end value the house-builder arrives at a residual figure (hence the name of the method) which is what he can afford to pay for the site. Alternatively, the builder may estimate the likely cost of the site, based on other land sales in the area, and arrive at an estimated level of profitability which may or may not be acceptable.

Table 7.1 is based on an actual profit statement undertaken for a housing site of 6 ha gross (5 ha net).

The first five rows summarise the 'site costs' of the project. Row 1 indicates the cost of buying the land, including any legal costs such as stamp duty and solicitors' fees. The site works figure represents the cost of clearing the site and putting in estate roads and sewers. The third row deals with estate completion costs, for example, agents' fees. Finally, there are 'extra-over' costs which are infrastructure costs over and above the normal costs of providing roads and sewers within a site. They are detailed in the bottom left hand column and in this case comprised a contribution for public open space (POS); a payment for maintaining a balancing pond; demolition of an existing property on the site; the unusually high cost of bringing water and gas supplies to the site; contribution to constructing the balancing pond; and the extra cost of special foundations because of poor ground conditions.

The next part of the table deals with the income and costs from house construction. Column 1 lists the 11 different house types (A–K) proposed on the site; column 2 indicates the number of houses of each type which the developer proposes. Column 3 gives the estimated selling price of each house. Column 4 allocates the site cost of each house by means of an agreed formula. This formula states that the site cost attributable to a house is proportional to the length of its frontage. Thus, house type B has a much wider frontage than house type K and it bears a heavier cost. Column 5 gives the construction costs per house and column 6 is the total of columns 4 and 5. Column 7 is the profit on each house, that is, the difference between column 3 and column 6 and the final column expresses the percentage profitability of each house type. In the present example the large houses, house types A, C and E were less profitable than the medium size properties (F and G).

The total row at the foot of this section of the table covers a number of points. First of all, it adds up the number of units (houses) in column 2 to give the total, that is, 126 units. In column 3 it multiplies the number of particular units by its sale price, doing this for each unit, and gives the sum of these multiplications, namely £9 996 000. Thus, the sales price total of £9 996 000 is the sum of 10 x £104 000, 10 x £95 000, and so on. A similar sequence of calculations is done in respect of the site costs (column 4), construction costs (column 5) and total costs (column 6). Thus the total site cost is £4 594 000; total construction cost £3 416 000 and combined total cost is £8 010 000. The figure of £1 986 000 at the foot of column 7 is arrived at in a similar way; it is the sum of the products of column 2 and column 7. Finally, the figure of 19.9 per cent at the foot of column 8 is the average percentage profit of all the houses. The next two rows of the table are both averages of the previous columns. They cover the average selling price of the houses, their average cost, etc. The percentage row indicates the relative proportion of sale price which the site costs, etc. account for. Thus site costs were 46 per cent of the sales price, construction costs 34 per cent and profit just under 20 per cent. If the developer had been prepared to accept a profitability of 10 per cent he could have bid a proportionally higher figure for the land, or built a less profitable mix of houses.

The resultant figure represents the maximum that the purchaser can afford, whilst still giving himself a profit margin. For negotiating purposes he will of course start at a somewhat lower price. Furthermore, it is one thing for a purchaser to demonstrate to a vendor that a site is worth only £x million, based on his residual valuation, but the vendor may refer to a comparable sale where £1.5 x million was paid and that sets the level. Whilst the residual method is therefore a helpful technique for the purchaser in deciding what the property is worth, it is by no means a technique that will avoid the need for negotiation and debate. It is perhaps a means of deciding what a purchaser can afford rather than a valuation of a site, although clearly there is a close relationship between the two.

The residual method of valuation is the normal method of valuation used by developers. However, it is necessary to distinguish between the valuation of a site by an agent and the developer's assessment of the viability of development. On the one hand a row of shops may be valued at £1.5 million, whilst a redevelopment appraisal may indicate a residual value for the shops of £1 million. This could simply demonstrate that the site is not ripe for redevelopment.

Table 7.1   Land investment profit statement

	Total £	Per ha. net £	Per unit £		
Land (inc legal)	4 034 100	797 250	32 010	Gross area	6.07 ha
Site works	300 000	59 290	2 380	Net area	5.06 ha
Est. comp.	75 000	14 820	590	Units	126
E/O costs	185 000	36 560	1 460	Net density*	24.9
Total	4 594 100	907 920	36 460		

House type	No.	Sale Price £	Site Cost £	Const Cost £	Total Cost £	Gross Profit £	Profit-ability %
A	10	104 000	45 640	37 800	83 440	20 560	19.8
B	10	95 000	51 100	33 200	84 300	10 700	11.3
C	6	110 000	53 030	38 600	91 630	18 370	16.7
D	12	84 000	39 990	30 550	70 540	13 460	16.0
E	12	103 000	51 630	39 600	90 230	12 770	12.4
F	21	71 000	27 120	21 500	48 620	22 380	31.5
G	14	88 000	34 910	31 100	66 010	21 990	25.0
H	11	68 500	32 360	24 200	56 560	11 940	17.4
I	6	60 500	30 750	17 600	48 350	12 150	20.1

							*
J	10	62 500	30 750	19 500	50 250	12 250	19.6
K	14	45 599	21 590	13 600	35 190	10 310	22.7
Total £'000	126	9 996	4 594	3 416	8 010	1986	19.9
Average £:		79 329	36 460	27 107	63 568	15 761	
Average %		100.0	46.0	34.2	80.1	19.9	

Extra over cost	£'000	Source of information		
		Info		Date
POS prov sum	10			
Comm. sum bl. pond	10			
Demolition	15	Dev. brief		25/05/86
Water cont.	25	House mix		"
Gas	25	Sales price		"
Half cost of bl. pond.	10	Const. costs		01/86
Spcl. founds	90	Swks costs		01/86
		E/O costs		25/06/86
Total	185	EPS calc		24/07/86

* In dwellings per ha.

In the above example there is no reference to inflation, interest charges and the timing of the development. The example is simply an estimated profit statement. It is probably not significantly inaccurate because when it was prepared it was reasonable to assume that the cost of interest and increases in construction costs that might have occurred throughout the duration of the project would have been balanced by an increase in selling price when the house was finally sold. If the house sold for even more the builder would regard it as a windfall profit. On larger projects timing, inflation and interest can become very important and they are considered below.

The example, shown in Table 7.2 introduces the concept of time through the inclusion of interest charges in the calculation. Before we consider time it is necessary briefly to explain the relationship between rent, yield and capital value. In the example a projected office development is expected to give an annual rent of £561 000. The developer estimates that he can sell the scheme to a pension fund to show a yield of 7.5 per cent. If the pension fund was investing the same amount of money in, say, a bank account, it might expect to earn a higher return each year, perhaps 10–12 per cent at 1990 interest rate levels. Why is it prepared to invest in a property which offers a lower rate of return? Because it expects rents and the capital value to increase in the future. Investing through a bank account offers no such increase. A fund may therefore be prepared to accept a very low yield. Given that the fund knows the rent of the property and given its acceptance of a particular yield, it is possible to derive a capital value from the property. This is done by taking the reciprocal of the yield and multiplying it by the annual rental. The reciprocal is known in valuation terminology as *years' purchase*:

$$K = Y.P. \times Rent \quad \text{where } K = \text{capital value and } Y.P. = \text{years' purchase}$$
$$Y.P. = \frac{1}{Yield}$$

In the example in Table 7.2 the fund is prepared to accept a yield of 7.5 per cent, which is equivalent to 13.33 years' purchase. This gives a gross capital value of £7.48 million. Against this figure are set the various development costs. Site acquisition is assumed at £1.5 million. Construction costs are just over £3 million and professional fees are a further £430 000. The concept of time appears in the interest charges. They assume that two years elapse between acquisition of the site and

Table 7.2 Circle system – development appraisal, High Street, Newton

	%	£	£	£
Realised sales				
Gross rent		561 000 pa		
Less ground rent		0 pa		
Net rental income		561 000 pa		
Capitalisation	(yield 7.50)	X 13.33 YP		7 480 000
			GDV	7 480 000
Purchaser's costs	3.3 (gross)	243 100	NDV	7 236 900
				0
			Net realisation	7 236 900
Outlay				
Sale agent fees	1.0	72 369		
Sale legal fees		0	72 369	
Site purchase price (0.6 ha)		1 500 000	(2 500 000 per ha)	
Stamp duty	1.0	15 000		
Land acq. agent	1.0	15 000		
Land acq. legal		20 000		
Grd rent agt fee		0		
Grd rent lgl fee		0		

Table 7.2   Circle system – development appraisal, High Street, Newton (contd)

Town plan/survey		11 000	
Arrangement fee		0	1 561 000
Construction	1.0	3 000 000	
Contingency		30 000	
Demolition		5 000	
Site works/roads		20 000	
Fees			
Architect	6.0	181 800	
Quantity surveyor	2.0	60 600	
Struct. engineer	2.0	60 600	
Mech/elec eng	1.0	30 300	
Misc. fees		0	
Project manager	1.0	30 300	
Statutory costs		2 000	
Misc. costs		0	
Marketing		10 000	
Letting agent/legal		56 100	3 486 700
Extra costs		0	
Value added tax		0	

	%	£	£	£
Interest (site 15.0%, building 15.0%)				
Site (excl. void)	24.0 mths	534 597		
Building (s-curve)	18.0 mths	410 577		
Void	3.00 mths	222 254		
Offset interest		0		
			1 167 428	
Costs				6 287 497
Profit	**15.1%**			**949 403**

disposal of it. The compound interest charge on the site acquisition amounts to £534 597. The cost of construction is spread over 18 months and the interest charge accumulates to £410 577. There is a further time element namely a period of three months when the building stands empty and has not been purchased by anyone. At the end of three months it is assumed that the building is sold.

Taking these costs into account, at the end of the day the developer receives a profit of £949 000 or 15%. If the developer is prepared to accept a lower profit rate he can afford to pay more for the site. This can be readily calculated on a computer.

In order to minimise the amount of interest that he has to pay on a project, the developer will wish to stagger payments as much as possible and he may be able to achieve this in a number of ways. First of all he will not pay until the prospect of starting the development is fairly imminent. It may be convenient to relate payment to the grant of detailed planning permission on at least part of the site. This would be preferable to the grant of outline permission, since on a large site it could take several months to sort out details of roads, sewers, building designs, landscaping, etc.

Secondly, and this applies to larger sites, for example, those of more than 2 ha (5 acres), the developer will prefer to buy the site in stages. This is because it will take several years for the buying public to purchase all the houses he proposes to build, or in the case of a commercial development to let all the floorspace that is provided.

Let us take an example of a housing site of 8 ha (20 acres). Builder *X* reckons he can sell one house a week off the site, excluding two weeks at the Christmas period, based on his experience of previous building sites. He expects to build the houses at a density of 25 houses/ha (10 houses per acre). Therefore the total capacity of the site is 200 houses and the development period is four years. To put it another way, 2 ha (5 acres) of the site will not be developed for three years, another 2 ha (5 acres) will not be developed for two years, another 2 ha (5 acres) for 1, and only 2 ha (5 acres) will actually be developed in the first year. Ideally then, the builder will pay for 2 ha (5 acres) in the first year; then for another 2 ha (5 acres) in the second year, and so on. In this way the builder avoids tying up money in land which is producing no return. Given that the money could be put to alternative profitable uses or, if it had been borrowed, would impose an interest burden on the builder, then clearly he is better off by staging his purchase, where this is practicable.

The advantage to the builder is a disadvantage to the vendor. The latter does not receive all his money at the outset, nor is there any compensating capital gains advantage through staging of the sale. Capital Gains Tax liability arises at the time of all or part of the sale and there are restrictions against schemes for artificially dividing up a site to reduce CGT.

At the end of the day each party to the transaction will negotiate a price that reflects the characteristics, such as staged payments, of the transaction. In no way, though, does this invalidate the basic principle of the residual method of valuation that is chosen as a starting point for negotiation.

An example of the time factor in viability appraisal will illustrate the above points in a tolerably true-to-life way. XYZ Developments Ltd. wish to acquire a disused factory and redevelop it for 4 000 m² of B1 units. They do not have planning permission and the owner requires payment in full on the day that detailed permission is granted. How much can XYZ afford to pay the owner and still make a profit? To answer this question we need to make certain assumptions about costs, income, timing, etc. The following tables set out the estimated timing of the development and financial data:

Estimated Timetable

Month 1	Receipt of detailed permission Prepare Building Regulation Plans Bill of Quantities
Month 3	Obtain tenders for construction
Month 6	Start on site
Month 18	Completion of construction works
Month 24	Sale of 2 000 m² (20 000 square feet)
Month 30	Sale of 2 000 m² (20 000 square feet)

Financial data, as at Month 1

Building costs	£400/m² (£40 per square foot) Construction costs payable in four equal amounts, in arrears. No allowance for inflation
Interest costs	2% per annum compound
Disposal income	£1 000/m² (£100 per square foot)

In the light of this data it is possible to prepare a cash flow profile indicating for any moment in time throughout the project what the financial position will be.

A worked example, based on an office development, is given in Table 7.3 and it shows the effect of the timing of receipts and outgoings. The format is a 'spreadsheet' from a computer program of cash flow using the same basic data as in Table 7.2 but introducing the time factor.

The net capital value is £7 236 902 as before, but in the spreadsheet example it is not realised until month 28 when the remaining half of the office is sold. By contrast, land acquisition costs have been incurred in months 3, 6 and 12. Construction costs were incurred in months 9, 12, 15, 18, 21 and 24. All the interest on land acquisition and construction costs has been accumulating, to the extent that by month 21, just before the first half of the building is sold the developer is £5¼ million down. At the end of the day this turns into a profit of £1m or 22 per cent of completed development value.

The advantage of this type of approach is that it is very easy, with the aid of a computer program, to value a development site according to different 'what if?' assumptions. Suppose, for example, that the interest rate is 10 per cent rather than 15 per cent, or that the development can be sold to show a yield of 6.5 per cent rather than 7.5 per cent, or that building costs can be deferred by three months relative to when the building is sold. All these variables can be readily run through the computer and inform the developer of how they affect the value of the site. If the value of the site is fixed, then the program will tell the developer whether the project gives him a satisfactory profit and help in deciding whether to go forward on the site.

Another advantage of this type of approach is that it shows which factors have the most effect on the final profit. It may be that deferring building costs for three months does not greatly affect the profitability of a project whereas a 0.5 per cent rise in interest rates turns a profit into a loss. The analysis of these effects is called sensitivity analysis and is a very useful aid to decision making on a site. For example, it can be used to demonstrate how critical the price of a site is. The developer may be encouraged to pay a very full price for a site if the analysis demonstrated that a small increase in rental per sq.ft. or m^2 of the building would more than offset a significant increase in land cost.

It is often more convenient to bring all the cost revenues and future values back to a common base known as net present value (NPV). The advantage of doing so is that it enables one to compare different projects and investments against a common criterion. The Net Present Value represents the current value of the cash flow containing all current and future costs, incomes and values discounted back at a specific rate of interest. This permits the time–related comparison of different projects.

Comparison of alternative project and investments is also made by calculating the Internal Rate of Return, which is the rate of interest necessary to discount a cash flow to produce a Net Present Value of nil. This is particularly relevant to the comparison of development projects to other forms of investment.

Thus, the value of project A, spread over three years, may be compared with project B, which will be completed in 18 months. Alternatively, it can be used to assess a single project against a given yardstick such as the rate of interest, to indicate whether a project is viable or not. It is evident that a payment of £100 000 in a few years time is worth less than a payment of £100 000 today. The amount by which it is less can be simply calculated by discounted cash–flow analysis. The main factors to be taken into account are the rate of interest and the period of time over which the payment or outgoing has to be discounted. It is outside the scope of this book to deal with discounted cash flow in detail and there are numerous text books which very adequately explain the method, for example, David Isaac and Terry Steley, *Property Valuation Techniques* (Macmillan, 1991).

Although the stimulus for development is invariably the profit motive this may manifest itself in very different ways according to the circumstances of the developer. A retail developer/operator may wish to secure a development purely as a means to increasing retail sales turnover, the housebuilder may evaluate a site on whether it enables him to meet a given profit level; and the hotel developer may wish to establish a presence in a given area.

The financial evaluation of a development site should take into account whether particular incentives are available that may turn a non-viable project into a viable one. It is not possible to give a detailed appraisal of the various incentives available, but the following summarises the main forms of assistance relevant to development proposals.

The Department of the Environment gives financial assistance to private sector developers in the form of City Grant, instituted in 1988. This replaced the previous types of grant known as Urban Development Grant, Urban Regeneration Grant and Derelict Land Grant in the 57 areas participating in the Department of the Environment's Urban

Table 7.3   Cash Flow Spreadsheet

MONTH NO/DATE Item	Amount	000:APR'90 TOTAL QTRLY B/F	003:JUL'90	006:OCT'90 -561 288	009:JAN'91 -1 111 461
NET CAP. RENT	7 236 902	0	0	0	0
SALE AGENT FEES	-72 369	0	0	0	0
PURCHASE PRICE	-1 500 000	0	-500 000	-500 000	0
STAMP DUTY	115 000	0	-5 000	-5 000	0
SITE AGENT FEES	-15 000	0	-5 000	-5 000	0
SITE LEGAL FEES	-20 000	0	-20 000	0	0
TOWN PLAN	-10 000	0	-10 000	0	0
SURVEY	-1 000	0	-1 000	0	0
CONSTRUCTION	-3 000 000	0	0	0	-218 201
CONTINGENCY	-30 000	0	0	0	-2 182
DEMOLITION	-5 000	0	0	0	-5 000
SITE WORKS/ROADS	-20 000	0	0	0	-20 000
ARCHITECT	-181 800	0	0	0	-13 223
QUANT. SURVEYOR	-60 600	0	0	0	-4 408
STR. ENGINEER	-60 600	0	0	0	-4 408
M/E ENGINEER	-30 300	0	0	0	-2 204
PROJECT MANAGER	-30 000	0	0	0	-2 204
STATUTORY COSTS	-2 000	0	0	0	-2 000
MARKETING	-10 000	0	0	0	0
LETTING AGENT	-56 100	0	0	0	0

VAT PAID	0	0	0
VAT RECOVERED	0	0	0
QUARTERLY TOTAL	0	−541 000	−510 000
DEBIT RATE (1) %PA		15.00	15.00
CREDIT RATE (1) %PA		15.00	15.00
INTEREST AMOUNT			
PER QUARTER		−20 288	−40 173
TOTAL C/F @			
QTRLY PERIOD	0	−561 288	−1 111 461

VAT PAID	0
VAT RECOVERED	0
QUARTERLY TOTAL	−273 829
DEBIT RATE (1) %PA	15.00
CREDIT RATE (1) %PA	15.00
INTEREST AMOUNT	
PER QUARTER	−47 719
TOTAL C/F @	
QTRLY PERIOD	−1 433 008

TABLE 7.3 (contd.)

	012:APR'91 -1 422 008	015:JUL'91 -2 602 220	018:OCT'91 -3 468 102	021:JAN'92 -4 395 854	024:APR'92 -5 235 249
NET CAP. RENT	0	0	0	0	3 618 451
SALE AGENT FEES	0	0	0	0	0
PURCHASE PRICE	-500 000	0	0	0	0
STAMP DUTY	-5 000	0	0	0	0
SITE AGENT FEES	-5 000	0	0	0	0
SITE LEGAL FEES	0	0	0	0	0
TOWN PLAN	0	0	0	0	0
SURVEY	0	0	0	0	0
CONSTRUCTION	-506 357	-662 937	-687 937	-581 358	-343 210
CONTINGENCY	-5 064	-6 629	-6 879	-5 814	-3 432
DEMOLITION	0	0	0	0	0
SITE WORKS/ROADS	0	0	0	0	0
ARCHITECT	-30 685	-40 174	-41 689	-35 230	-20 799
QUANT. SURVEYOR	-10 228	-13 391	-13 896	-11 743	-6 933
STR. ENGINEER	-10 228	-13 391	-13 896	-11 743	-6 933
M/E ENGINEER	-5 114	-6 696	-6 948	-5 872	-3 466
PROJECT MANAGER	-5 114	-6 696	-6 948	-5 872	-3 466
STATUTORY COSTS	0	0	0	0	0
MARKETING	0	0	0	0	0
LETTING AGENT	0	0	0	0	0

VAT PAID	0	0	0	0	0
VAT RECOVERED	0	0	0	0	0
QUARTERLY TOTAL	-1 082 791	-749 914	-778 194	-657 632	-3 230 212
DEBIT RATE (1) %PA	15.00	15.00	15.00	15.00	15.00
CREDIT RATE (1) %PA	15.00	15.00	15.00	15.00	15.00
INTEREST AMOUNT PER QUARTER	-86 421	-115 967	-149 558	-181 763	-71,257
TOTAL C/F @ QTRLY PERIOD	-2 602 220	-3 468 102	-4 395 854	5 235 249	-2 076 294

Table 7.3 (contd.)

	027:JUL'92 −2 076 294	028:AUG'92 −2 154 155
NET CAP. RENT	0	3 618 451
SALE AGENT FEES	0	−72 369
PURCHASE PRICE	0	0
STAMP DUTY	0	0
SITE AGENT FEES	0	0
SITE LEGAL FEES	0	0
TOWN PLAN	0	0
SURVEY	0	0
CONSTRUCTION	0	0
CONTINGENCY	0	0
DEMOLITION	0	0
SITE WORKS/ROADS	0	0
ARCHITECT		
QUANT. SURVEYOR	0	0
STR. ENGINEER	0	0
M/E ENGINEER	0	0
PROJECT MANAGER	0	0
STATUTORY COSTS	0	0
MARKETING		−10 000
LETTING AGENT	0	−56 100

VAT PAID	0	0
VAT RECOVERED		0
QUARTERLY TOTAL		3 279 892
DEBIT RATE (1) %PA	15.00	0.00
CREDIT RATE (1) %PA	15.00	0.00
INTEREST AMOUNT PER		
QUARTER	−77 861	0
TOTAL C/F @	−2 154 155	
QTRLY PERIOD		1 325 827

CASH FLOW RESULTS

TOTAL REVENUE	7 236 902
TOTAL COSTS	−5 120 069
TOTAL VAT	0
TOTAL INTEREST	−791 006
PROFIT	1 325 827
PROFIT %	22 43%

NPV %	0%
NPV TARGET	2 116 833
IRR	38.8%

(IRR EXCLUDES INTEREST)

ASSUMPTIONS

VAT PERIOD 3 MONTHS
INTEREST COMPOUNDED QUARTERLY
INTEREST CHARGED MONTHLY
PAYMENTS IN ADVANCE
RECEIPTS IN ADVANCE

Programme and which are listed in Appendix 3. The purpose of the grant is, in the words of the Department: to bridge the gap between development costs and values on completion, enabling the developer to make a reasonable return.

(See Department of Environment 'Reviewing the Cities'. A report on the Department of Environment Inner City Programme in 1989–1990. (DOE 1990.) Criteria for the allocation of Grant are that the project value exceeds £200 000 and that the project assists urban regeneration, for example, by bringing derelict land into use, creating local employment, etc. Developments which can benefit from Grant include housing, offices, factories and commercial uses. On average the amount of grant that may be payable is about 20 per cent to 25 per cent of the total development costs incurred by the developer and grants have been in the range of about £200 000 to several million pounds. Recent examples include the grant of £224 000 towards the construction of 32 houses, workshops and offices on a derelict 0.8-ha (2-acre) site in Middlesborough; and £78 000 towards construction of two industrial buildings in Hartlepool.

Grants can also be obtained from the European Community under the European Regional Development Fund. For example the Fund gave £53 000 towards North East Derbyshire District Council's site development costs at an industrial estate in Killamarsh, already the recipient of £47 000 from the same fund. The money will help towards the cost of drainage and service installations. The Departments of the Environment and Transport also make grants available under the Industrial Development Act (1982) towards essential improvements to infrastructure.

Derelict Land Grant is still available outside the 57 Urban Programme areas. The amount payable varies throughout the country according to whether the site is in an Assisted Area, a Derelict Land Clearance Area or otherwise. As an indication of the scale of Derelict Land Grant, the Department of the Environment had a DLG budget of £71.5 million throughout the country for the year 1990/91 and allocated £1.9 million to Corby District Council alone in that year.

Enterprise Zones

There are 26 Enterprise Zones in the United Kingdom; those in England and Wales are shown on Plan 1, and vary in size from 48 to 440 ha. In these zones developers can claim tax allowances on capital expenditure involved in the development. The tax allowance reduces the real costs of development but it is not an allowance which is available to institutional funds. For this reason the Enterprise Zones have attracted private not institutional investment money. Although there are financial advantages to developing in Enterprise Zones, the relaxed planning regime is held by many who have developed in such zones to be a more important advantage.

8 Drawing the Evaluation Together

The evaluation of development sites involves several strands of activity which can be time-consuming and expensive. A soil survey could cost a thousand pounds or more, as could a planning report. Ideally the developer wishes to obtain all the relevant information as quickly as possible so that he has a thorough understanding of all aspects of the project on which to take a decision. How he achieves this will depend on the circumstances in which the developer gets to know of the site.

One technique is to carry out a planning study first that will show which sites in a given area might be suitable, in planning terms, for development. The developer then tries to find out the owners of each site and, if the owner is willing to sell, he, the developer, will carry out further investigations, of legal charges, ground conditions and so on. This approach has been much used by housebuilders looking for greenfield sites in a district or county.

Alternatively, the developer may have identified one specific site or property in a built-up area which he feels has development potential. In this case he will wish to get a planner's/surveyor's opinion on the potential and, if it has potential, he will contact the owner.

A third possibility is where the site is introduced to the developer. Either the owner or his agent may approach the developer direct, for example because the developer is well known in the area or he may be known personally to the agent. Or else the site is put on the open market and developers are invited to make offers for it. Either way the developer's main preoccupation will be with assessing the planning potential and perhaps physical characteristics of the site. It seems very unlikely that a site would be offered by the owner if there were legal restrictions on its development. To some extent also the planning potential should have been considered by the landowner before offering it to a developer since it is the development potential that creates value for the landowner. Whether the landowner will have undertaken such an exercise depends on his resources and the cost of establishing the planning potential.

A preliminary planning appraisal can be undertaken fairly quickly and at no great expense, to establish whether a site has any potential or none. Part of this preliminary exercise should include a site visit.

It is almost always worth visiting the site or property even when time is at a premium. A practical tip is to take photographs of a site at the time it is visited. It is surprising how one may easily forget certain factors of a site, for example, was there a hedgerow on one boundary, was a shop vacant or trading? Taking photographs should only be contemplated, though, if it can be done without causing offence or suspicion. On occasions it will be very undiplomatic to photograph, say, a factory which is in business if the intention is to acquire it for redevelopment. It is likely that the workforce will not be aware of the redevelopment possibility and they could become very suspicious or unsettled at the sight of a photographer. Nevertheless, where it can be achieved a photographic record will assist the myriad details that the visitor thinks he has recorded but on occasion may have omitted. The record is especially useful when presenting an appraisal of a site to another person who has not visited it because he does not carry any impression of the site at all.

It is essential both to visit the site and take careful notes of the visit. The notes should describe the usage of the property, means of access, physical features, for example, overhead power line, the general character of the area, any uses that may not have shown up in the general particulars of the site, location of statutory undertakers apparatus both on or adjoining the site. It is true that this information can be obtained from other sources, for example, the local authority, or statutory undertakers and the information may be more comprehensive than one can glean from a site visit. However, the site visit provides instant information, whereas a more exhaustive study could take weeks or months.

Obviously, the time and date of a site visit can be important and should therefore be recorded. This is particularly true if one is appraising a retail opportunity. Market day in a small country town may produce a very different impression of retail potential in a street compared with a non-market day. Or the possibility of a traffic problem affecting a site may not be apparent on a Sunday afternoon, whereas on a weekday there could be evidence of severe traffic congestion. This would have a direct bearing on whether or not a development proposal would have to include off-site road works.

The preliminary appraisal should give some idea of whether a site is a complete 'no hoper', or whether its development can be confidently assumed. In practice, of course, most sites fall somewhere in between these two extremes; for example, a site may be 'white land' on the edge of a town, of average agricultural quality but subject to a general planning policy of restraint. If, however, the planning appraisal is not categorically pessimistic the developer may wish to go further with technical appraisals, for example, of ground conditions, etc. It is possible that the developer can avoid this stage if his deal with the landowner is worded in such a way that 'abnormal' development costs are deducted from the sale price of the property. For example, poor ground conditions might result in additional foundation costs of £100 000.Or it may be necessary to construct a pumping station and rising main for £50 000 more than conventional gravity sewers could cost. This need not be a problem, provided that the developer has built it into the agreement.

Let us assume that the planning potential has been established and that the landowner can demonstrate that there are no legal impediments to development. The evaluation exercise then centres on just the following factors:

1 Physical characteristics
2 Marketing
3 Viability

In practice the developer often has to take decisions without full information – perhaps a vendor has imposed a very tight deadline – and the developer may then have to put the information and advice he requires in some sort of order. The following remarks offer some advice on this aspect.

Perhaps the most fundamental aspect of all is establishing ownership. It is no good satisfying oneself that planning permission could be obtained for the desired scheme if part of the site proves to be in the ownership of a third party. Therefore, it is of the utmost importance to be sure that the vendor is in fact the freehold owner of the property, or whatever he claims to be, for example, a long leaseholder. Under the heading of ownership one should include any restrictive covenants which could undermine the feasibility of the proposed scheme.

Viability, of which marketing may be regarded as a subsidiary aspect, is especially important, since a developer will not undertake a project which does not show a profit. A good example of the interplay of ownership and viability can be seen in Swindon.

Plan 14a shows an area of central Swindon as it was in about 1970. Plan 14b shows the same area in 1990, where there are now several recent office developments. On the old plan Cheltenham and Gloucester Streets were lined with terraced houses on both sides. A builder's merchant lay between the two streets, facing Station Road and occupied what used to be another terrace of housing.

The builder's merchant was in one ownership but the terraced houses in Cheltenham and Gloucester Streets were in separate ownerships until the late 1960s. A developer began to acquire ownership of the terraced houses over a period of years. Once acquired, a house would be let out to provide a continuing income to the developer, but it was an income that bore no relationship to the potential income that would result from an office development. At the same time as completing the assembly of the houses the developer obtained planning permission for offices (this was in the early 1970s) and the area has been redeveloped as several office buildings which are now occupied.

An earlier stage in the same process can be seen in Morley Street, Swindon. This street was an extensive area of terraced housing in about 1965 to 1970 (see Plan 14c), but the area has been transformed by construction of the Brunel Shopping Centre immediately to the north. The properties in Havelock Street were shops in 1960 and remain so. All the properties in Granville Street and the west side of Morley street were assembled by developers and subsequently acquired by the local authority and cleared to make a surface car park. The east side of Morley Street, originally in residential use, has become commercial in character but has not yet been redeveloped, although land assembly by developers has occurred (see Plan 14d). Gradually, the two ingredients of an urban development site will be present, namely, single ownership (or at least a common agreement to develop by several owners); and, secondly, viability. When these ingredients are present, the site can be looked on as a development site.

The evaluation of a development site should result in a decision on whether a particular development is worth pursuing or not. It should also indicate whether a development is worth pursuing now, or at some future date. Thus the analysis may indicate that a retail scheme for example would be appropriate but, because of high borrowing charges at present or currently depressed consumer spending, the scheme should be put on ice for a year or two.

This is a commercial judgement which goes well beyond town

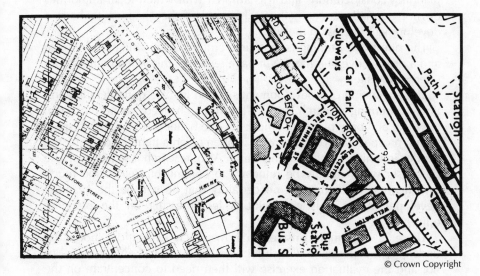

(a)   (b)

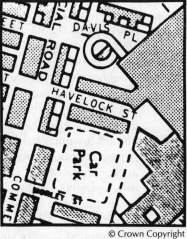

(c)   (d)

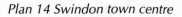

Plan 14 Swindon town centre

planning considerations and it is an area with which local authorities do not normally concern themselves unless they happen to have a development interest in the site.

The question of timing is of course crucial to the valuation of a site and a prospective purchaser will have regard to this when he makes an offer for the site.

The evaluation of a development site can involve quite detailed and time-consuming research. Ideally the research needs to be thorough; the local authority planning officer may be better placed in this respect than a prospective purchaser who is often given a tight deadline by the vendor in which to make up his mind. Also, research is expensive. The purchaser will naturally be reluctant to commit himself to too much investigation when there is no certainty that he will be the eventual developer. Again, this constraint is less pressing on the planning officer.

There is no simple answer to how much evaluation should be undertaken. Experience will show whether a site has any potential or not and the evaluation exercise will then need to concentrate on the following areas:

1 Exactly how much development of a particular type can be achieved; for example, a 6-storey office building with 40 parking spaces as against a 3-storey building. Or, 1.6 ha (4 acres) of housing and 0.4 ha (1 acre) of open space as against 1.8 ha (4.5 acres) of housing and 0.2 ha (0.5 acre) of open space.

2 Technical evaluation. This can often be simplified by reference to other development in the vicinity. For example, the ground conditions of a site are unlikely to be problematic if the site is on the same level as development which surrounds it and there does not appear to have been any tipping or underground workings in the past. Of course, this is only an educated guess and when time permits it will probably be necessary to undertake a proper ground survey. It should be noted, incidentally, that a sloping site may appear suitable for development and be surrounded by other developments, yet the underlying strata may be totally unsuitable for building on. For example, in the Old Town area of Swindon, which lies on a hill to the south of the town centre, there is an underground layer of shifting sand. Because of this layer there are parts of Old Town which cannot readily be built on, except perhaps by piling through the sand stratum. These areas adjoin

perfectly stable areas for building, but just happen to be where the sand stratum comes near the surface.

Where the developer is already the owner of the property the situation is different. He may himself undertake the evaluation exercise and any subsequent planning application. In these circumstances there is less need to put priorities on the evaluation tasks and the more important issue is whether the landowner should undertake the work himself or invite a developer to do so.

9 Conclusions

The evaluation of development sites is an important activity both for
the developer and the local authority, albeit for different reasons. The
developer will be anxious to establish as accurately as possible the
extent of the development potential of a site. The evaluation exercise is
designed to help him in this task. It may show that planning permission
has actually been given for the development which he would wish to
undertake; in this case the developer will know that the town planning
aspect of the evaluation is certain and he need apply his judgement
and experience solely to legal, financial and marketing matters. Very
often the planning position will not be clear and the developer may
need to allow considerable time and effort in settling it.

Although the developer will in due course know what the planning
and legal position is with some certainty, he must at the end of the day
take a risk that his proposed development will find a customer, whether
it be a house buyer, retailer or office tenant. No amount of evaluation
can wholly remove this risk. This does not mean that the evaluation
exercise is pointless. Apart from clearing up the planning, legal and
technical aspects of a site the evaluation should also give the developer
a good idea of the market for his product. The evaluation should for
example tell him whether to build starter homes in an area or 4
bedroom detached houses; or whether small office suites are attractive
to users rather than a large office building with extensive floor areas, or
whether the building should be air conditioned.

The decision to develop is a very important one because it involves
large sums of money. It is clearly desirable to carry out the sort of
evaluation described in this book before taking the development decision and, arguably, anyone lending money to a developer or agreeing
in advance to buy the finished product from him, will require a
detailed evaluation of the site and project as a precondition of the
finance.

However, there is the danger, so far as the developer is concerned,

127

that too much evaluation could lose the site. At times a developer must act quickly because he is competing with other prospective purchasers of a site. He may not be able to carry out a thorough examination of the site and he has to select the most important features of the evaluation that are consistent with his timetable.

A risk attaches to such expediency, but it is a risk that may be quite acceptable especially in a strong market. Many housebuilders acquired development sites in the second half of the 1980s without a careful financial evaluation but, as land and house prices were increasing rapidly at the time, any mistakes would be quickly ironed out. The difficulty arose later when sites purchased at the top of the market then plummeted in value at the end of the decade, rendering the previous evaluation of their viability quite meaningless.

The reasons for the local authority undertaking the evaluation exercise are rather different, but they do not thereby make it any less important. The local authority is not so preoccupied with selecting sites whose developments will make a profit. Its concern is inter alia to allocate land uses to sites which make sense in land-use planning terms. Thus the town planner drafting a local plan for his area will wish to evaluate different sites for new development and the evaluation exercise will lead him to reject some sites and select others for particular forms of development. This approach works well in the case of greenfield sites; the planner can probably judge quite well whether field A is preferable to field B in planning terms. Increasingly, he may have to consider whether one already developed site is preferable to another and this brings different types of planning judgement into play.

Previously-developed land should only be considered when it is genuinely available. However, if it is available there is a clear planning preference to use such land rather than greenfield sites.

In the preparation of a local plan this is a valid activity for the planner to get involved in, since one of the functions of the plan is to allocate land for development which the planners judge to be needed in an area.

The evaluation exercise, then, is quite different for the local authority planner drawing up his/her local plan, compared to the developer. The former, having estimated the land requirements of various types of development that are needed in the plan area, will evaluate certain sites which could meet those needs. He/she discharges his task by identifying enough land, and probably no more, to meet the particular requirements. The developer on the other hand is mainly concerned to evaluate a particular site rather than a range of sites.

Because they have different objectives the local authority planner and the developer will look at different matters when undertaking an evaluation. Broadly speaking, the local authority planner should have regard solely to town planning matters in his evaluation whilst the developer must concern himself with profitability and marketing as well as town planning. Despite their different outlooks the town planning element is a common theme. While the local authority and developer will not necessarily see eye to eye on the planning merits of a particular site, it is very desirable for the developer to evaluate the planning aspects carefully. It is more likely that sound planning will evolve as a result of such examination.

It is not difficult to identify a good site for development. In the case of greenfield sites the obvious place to look is on the edges of towns, cities and villages. Having identified a possible site one has to go through the detailed planning evaluation to test its suitability in more detail. The developer will also undertake a financial and marketing evaluation.

Redevelopment sites are less readily identifiable but usually involve the replacement of one or more buildings with new ones that either result in enhanced development value (where the developer is promoting the site) or a town planning or community objective (where the local authority is promoting the site). The two alternatives are not mutually exclusive.

If it is a relatively easy matter to identify a site, why are some developments and local authorities more successful than others? From a developer's standpoint part of the skill lies in knowing the market. This may be interpreted widely. First he needs to know the owners of the property, to be in the right place at the right time; and secondly, he needs to know what sort of product is wanted by the market. This does not come from carrying out site evaluation exercises, however carefully. It comes from regular contact with occupiers and their agents. This is true whether his product is an office, a shop or a house. Another aspect, which this book has barely touched upon, but which can be critical to the success of a development is the ability to devise a suitable financing scheme. The developer who understands the variety of ways of financing a project will have the edge on a purchaser whose only source of finance is his bank. An accountant, and probably tax lawyer, can be crucial in understanding this complex aspect of development.

The local authority will be judged successful when it can identify a site for a particular use that not only meets its town planning objectives but also is acceptable to the market. However, the market is not a simple, definable entity but is always changing. In a strong market a site may be attractive to developers and in a weak market it stands undeveloped. For this very reason the local authority should not, by and large, be influenced too much by the state of the market at a particular point in time. This may leave the local authority in a dilemma. Should it put forward proposals for development, unswayed by current market conditions? If it does, it may risk criticism for being 'unrealistic'. At best its proposals may simply remain on the plan without being put into effect. There is no short answer to this difficulty but as a guiding principle perhaps local authorities should err on the side of caution. Once built a building may be around for decades, whereas market conditions can change in a matter of months. Therefore, the planning authority has a particular responsibility to take a reasonably long-term view of things.

This is not to say that the development industry will thank a local authority for taking a long time to evaluate various development sites, for example, in its local planning work or in preparing a development brief. What the industry is looking for is speed, clarity and fairness. Evaluation should not take years, notwithstanding the need for public scrutiny and accountability; the reasons for the choice of one site rather than another should be clear to the industry and the public. Finally, the choice should be fair and not influenced by whether for example, a site is in a local authority's ownership or not.

Public interest in development has never been greater than at present; the cost of land has assumed a greater proportion of total development costs than ever before; the importance of obtaining planning permission has never been greater in the mind of the developer. For all these reasons the need for sympathetic, effective and expeditious site evaluation is widely recognised and it is a need which is going to increase with time.

Appendix 1 Reference Sources

Department of the Environment

1 Circular 42/55MHLG   Green Belts
2 Circular 50/57MHLG   Green Belts
3 Circular 14/84DOE   Green Belts
4 Circular 15/84DOE   Land for Housing
5 Circular 22/84 & Memorandum on Structure and Local Plans
6 Circular 16/87 DOE   Development Involving
                                Agricultural Land
7 Circular 21/87 DOE   Contaminated Land
8 Planning Policy Guidance Notes,
  Regional Planning Guidances Notes
  Minerals Planning Guidance Notes
9 Index of Current Planning Guidance 1990

The Future of Development Plans: Cmnd 569 HMSO

Appendix 2 Agricultural Land Classification

Description of the Grades and Subgrades

The ALC grades and subgrades are described below in terms of the types of limitation which can occur, typical cropping range and the expected level and consistency of yield. In practice, the grades are defined by reference to physical characteristics and the grading guidance and cut-offs for limitation factors in Section 3 enable land to be ranked in accordance with these general descriptions. The most productive and flexible land falls into Grades 1 and 2 and Subgrade 3a and collectively comprises about one-third of the agricultural land in England and Wales. About half the land is of moderate quality in Subgrade 3b or poor quality in Grade 4. Although less significant on a national scale such land can be locally valuable to agriculture and the rural economy where poorer farmland predominates. The remainder is very poor quality land in Grade 5, which mostly occurs in the uplands.

Descriptions are also given of other land categories which may be used on ALC maps.

Grade 1 – excellent quality agricultural land

Land with no or very minor limitations to agricultural use. A very wide range of agricultural and horticultural crops can be grown and commonly includes top fruit, soft fruit, salad crops and winter harvested vegetables. Yields are high and less variable than on land of lower quality.

Grade 2 – very good quality agricultural land

Land with minor limitations which affect crop yield, cultivations or harvesting. A wide range of agricultural and horticultural crops can usually be grown but on some land in the grade there may be reduced flexibility due to difficulties with the production of the more demanding crops such as winter harvested vegetables and arable root crops. The level of yield is generally high but may be lower or more variable than Grade 1.

Grade 3 – good to moderate quality agricultural land

Land with moderate limitations which affect the choice of crops, timing and type of cultivation, harvesting or the level of yield. Where more demanding crops are grown yields are generally lower or more variable than on land in Grades 1 and 2.

Subgrade 3a – good quality agricultural land
Land capable of consistently producing moderate to high yields of a narrow range of arable crops, especially cereals, grass, oilseed rape, potatoes, sugar beet and the less demanding horticultural crops.

Subgrade 3b – moderate quality agricultural land
Land capable of producing moderate yields of a narrow range of crops, principally cereals and grass or lower yields of a wider ranger of crops or high yields of grass which can be grazed or harvested over most of the year.

Grade 4 – poor quality agricultural land

Land with severe limitations which significantly restrict the range of crops and/or level of yields. It is mainly suited to grass with occasional arable crops (e.g. cereals and forage crops) the yields of which are variable. In moist climates, yields of grass may be moderate to high but there may be difficulties in utilisation. The grade also includes very droughty arable land.

Grade 5 – very poor quality agricultural land

Land with very severe limitations which restrict use to permanent pasture or rough grazing, except for occasional pioneer forage crops.

Description of Other Land Categories used on ALC Maps

Urban

Built-up or 'hard' uses with relatively little potential for a return to agriculture including: housing, industry, commerce, education, transport, religious buildings, cemeteries. Also, hard-surfaced sports facilities, permanent caravan sites and vacant land; all types of derelict land, including mineral workings which are only likely to be reclaimed using Derelict Land Grants.

Non-agricultural

'Soft' uses where most of the land could be returned relatively easily to agriculture, including: golf courses, private parkland, public open spaces, sports fields, allotments and soft-surfaced areas on airports/ airfields. Also active mineral workings and refuse tips where restoration conditions to 'soft' after-uses may apply.

Woodland

Includes commercial and non-commercial woodland. A distinction may be made as necessary between farm and non-farm woodland.

Agricultural buildings

Includes the normal range of agricultural buildings as well as other relatively permanent structures such as glasshouses. Temporary structures (e.g. polythene tunnels erected for lambing) may be ignored.

Open water

Includes lakes, ponds and rivers as map scale permits.

Land not surveyed

Agricultural land which has not been surveyed.

Where the land use includes more than one of the above land cover types, e.g. buildings in large grounds, and where map scale permits, the cover types may be shown separately. Otherwise, the most extensive cover type will usually be shown.

Appendix 3   Urban Programme Authorities as at 1990

North West Region

Blackburn
Bolton
Burnley
Manchester
Oldham
Preston
Rochdale
Salford
Wigan

Merseyside Task Force Area

Halton
Knowsley
Liverpool
Sefton
St Helens
Wirral

South West Region

Bristol
Plymouth

Northern Region

Gateshead
Hartlepool
Langbaurgh
Middlesbrough
Newcastle
North Tyneside
South Tyneside
Stockton
Sunderland

West Midlands Region

Birmingham
Coventry
Dudley
Sandwell
Walsall
Wolverhampton
The Wrekin

East Midlands Region

Derby
Leicester
Nottingham

Yorkshire and Humberside Region

Barnsley
Bradford
Doncaster
Kingston-upon-Hull
Kirklees
Leeds
Rotherham
Sheffield

London Region

Brent
Greenwich
Hackney
Hammersmith & Fulham
Haringey
Islington
Kensington & Chelsea
Lambeth
Lewisham
Newham
Southwark
Tower Hamlets
Wandsworth

Index